LEAP INTO HR CONSULTING®

HOW TO MOVE **SUCCESSFULLY** FROM CORPORATE TO **CONSULTING**

SARAH HAMILTON-GILL FCIPD

Copyright © 2025 by Sarah Hamilton-Gill. All rights reserved.

This book or any portion thereof may not be reproduced or used in any manner whatsoever without the express written permission of the publisher except for the use of brief quotations in a book review.

Strenuous attempts have been made to credit all copyrighted materials used in this book. All such materials and trademarks, which are referenced in this book, are the full property of their respective copyright owners. Every effort has been made to obtain copyright permission for material quoted in this book. Any omissions will be rectified in future editions.

This book is written for information only – purely based on the opinion, personally acquired knowledge and experiences and point of view of the author – and does not claim to provide professional advice.

You take full responsibility for the actions you take following these recommendations mentioned here.

The author and publisher make no warranties, either expressed or implied, concerning the applicability, accuracy, reliability, or suitability of the contents of this book.

The author and the publisher of this book shall in no event be held liable for any direct, indirect, incidental, or consequential damages arising directly or indirectly from the use of any of the information contained within this book.

Cover image by: Gus Tyk, 99Designs
Book design by: SWATT Books Ltd

Printed in the United Kingdom
First Printing, 2020
Second Edition, 2025

ISBN: 978-1-8382365-3-3 (Black & White Paperback)
ISBN: 978-1-8382365-4-0 (Full Colour Paperback)
ISBN: 978-1-8382365-5-7 (eBook)

Sarah Hamilton-Gill
Lymington, Hampshire
SO41 0FD

www.leapintoconsulting.com

Dedication

I dedicate this book to you, so that through self-discovery you will gain confidence, clarity, and the motivation to take the next steps into HR consulting. You'll learn what is holding you back and become empowered to be more creative and productive and begin to live a life with more passion and purpose.

Each stage of the book takes you on a journey and builds your foundations for achieving your goals and ambitions.

This book is dedicated to those that recognise the awesomeness of their dreams and are searching for a more heart-centred and authentic life.

I dedicate this book to all those that have been part of my journey, my clients, colleagues, business partners, coaches. and my family.

I especially want to thank my two sons Aaron and Guy without whom I wouldn't have had the drive or need tc succeed, in the early days.

There are many influences in my business life, and I don't want to sound like an Oscar speech so I'd like to thank the whole team that makes the whole business happen.

You all know how you have contributed to my success.

Lastly, I want to thank from the bottom of my heart my partner who tells me he is so proud of me and with whom I wish to continue to share our future dreams together here in Corfu.

Onwards and upwards!

Sarah

> "Whatever you do, or dream you can, begin it. Boldness has genius and power and magic in it."
> *Johann Wolfgang von Goethe*

Contents

Dedication	3
Introduction	11
How to use this book	12
My Story	14
Living the dream	14
My early story	16

PART 1: Why you, why now? — 25

Chapter 1: Why now?	26
The business landscape	27
The consulting market	29
The key findings from the CIPD LinkedIn group survey	35
Chapter 2: Why you?	43
What is your current scenario	43
Chapter 3: Your future story	61
Be paid for the expertise that you already have	62
Creating a better work–life balance	66
Chapter 4: What is consulting?	68
Why use consultants?	68

The perception of a consultant	69
Outsourced strategic projects	70
Variety is the spice of life	71

Chapter 5: Is consulting right for you? 72
Consulting isn't for everyone	72
What is the best profile for a consultant?	75
What is essential for success?	78
HR consultant 360-degree feedback questionnaire	86
Consulting cycle and skills	89

Chapter 6: The benefits of consulting 91

Chapter 7: What type of business do you want? 95
Do I need to be a Ltd business?	95
Contracting	97
Interim roles	98
HR Franchising as an Option for HR Professionals	100
Independent HR consultant	105

Chapter 8: Delivering larger projects and growing your business 107
Keep the end goal in sight	109
Growing pains	110
Work from home vs an office	111
Three growth drivers	114
Income Strategies	115

PART 2: The 5C's "From Corporate to Consulting" Model 117

Supercharge your chance of success	118
Why is it important to get quick wins?	119
The From Corporate to Consulting Model	120

Chapter 9: Confidence — 122
    Why is confidence important? — 123
    Confidence around your expertise — 129
    The Wheel of Life — 136

Chapter 10: Clarity — 139
    What's your why? — 142
    Who is your ideal client? — 156
    Your client's pain points — 159
    Bringing it all together — 166
    How do you charge for your services? — 167
    Pricing – Summary page — 174
    Where do you find your ideal clients? — 176

Chapter 11: Credibility — 179
    Your presence on social media — 182
    The Presence Platform Audit — 186
    Your Expert Positioning — 190
    Personal branding — 192
    Your value — 197
    Maximising your social media presence — 201
    Market research — 202
    Awards — 204

Chapter 12: Collaboration — 207
    Working with partners — 209
    Working with associates — 215

Chapter 13: Courage — 221
    Effective work habits — 224
    Taking the right actions — 233
    Giving it all away — 237
    Using systems to support your flexible business and increase productivity — 241

Automate to Elevate: How HR Consultants Can Ditch the Repetitive Tasks and Scale with Ease	247
Wellbeing and looking after yourself	250
Team support	256
My goals and accountability	257
Your weekly check-ins	260

PART 3: Preparing to Leave the Corporate World — 263

Chapter 14: When is a good time for you? — 264
What crossroads are you at?	266
Having the best of both worlds	269

Chapter 15: The change curve — 271
A mountain of concerns	274

Chapter 16: Creating an income from Day 1 — 275
So how do you create an income from Day 1?	275
Quick wins – getting your ideal clients	277

Chapter 17: You are thinking of resigning now! — 280
Top tips before you resign	280

PART 4: The First 12 Months of Your Business — 283

Chapter 18: The First Year of Running an HR Consultancy: The Highs, The Lows, and The Must-Do's — 284

Chapter 19: How to Find Clients as an HR Consultant (Without Losing Your Mind) — 287
- 20 Tried and Tested Ways to Get More Clients — 287
- Skills & Behaviours for Success in Finding Clients — 292
- Tools & Systems to Improve Conversion Rates — 295
- Regional Differences: UK, USA, Canada, Australia — 297
- The Business Development Cycle for HR Consultants: A Step-by-Step Guide — 300
- Your Next Steps — 312

PART 5: Living the Dream: The Next Level — 315

Chapter 18: Career transition stories from HR professionals who leaped — 316
- Story 1 – New challenges — 316
- Story 2 – Finding Your Niche — 321
- Story 3 – Scaling for Success — 326
- Story 4 – Flexibility — 331
- Story 5 – Carving My Own Path — 336
- Top tips about a career transition: — 340
- The Power of Feedback — 341

Chapter 19: Remember the dream — 343
- What is your dream? — 343

About the Author — 345

References and Thanks for Contributions — 348
- Additional Resources — 350

"The biggest risk you can take is to do nothing."

Brad Sugars

Introduction

Let's get straight to the point. You've bought this book because you want a change in your personal or professional life. Most likely you want a change in both.

Some people make the Leap into HR Consulting® because they want to work across more interesting and varied projects than working for one employer allows for. Others make the change to spend less time at a desktop and more time on holiday, or with loved ones. Most wish to achieve all of this, and more.

That's the great thing about becoming an HR consultant; you get to pick and choose what you wish to work on, when you want to do it, and how much time you spend in the (often virtual) office. You can even choose where that virtual office is.

You may well have picked up this book because you want to take more control over your future, your wealth, the work that you do, and how you get rewarded for your skills.

Leap into HR Consulting® has been written to help you to discover everything you need to learn before embarking on your journey of self-discovery to becoming a consultant.

Drawing on my extensive experience of running an HR consulting business, as well as creating a 360-degree feedback product that is now sold in over 56 countries, this motivational book has the power to help you discover your uniqueness and how you can use this to create your own consulting business and serve clients.

This book is for you if you are contemplating going into consulting having had a career in human resources or people related disciplines. You might be an HR manager, director, or work in people management in its broadest sense. It doesn't matter if you work in the public sector, private, or a charity, what matters is that you want to take control of your own destiny and enjoy the freedom and rewards that your new career will bring.

Leap into HR Consulting® will help you to recognise that you have the necessary experience to make this move, even if there is an element of self-doubt creeping in.

In this informative and practical book, you'll find the guidance and tools you need to take the Leap into HR Consulting®. Together we'll cover what you need to know in order to make it happen.

HOW TO USE THIS BOOK

There are four parts to this book.

In **Part 1**, I explore the role of a consultant, and what you need to know so that you can explore whether it's the right move for you.

Part 2 covers my model, The 5C's "From Corporate to Consulting" Model, providing you with insights, tips and knowledge about the world of independent consulting and showing you how you too can make the transition in a stress-free way.

In **Part 3**, If you are still employed, I give you advice and thoughts as you embark on your decision to leave.

In **Part 4**, I explore the key to being successful in your first year.

And in **Part 5**, I share honest stories of successful HR consultants and how their journeys started, so that you can see how much is possible by getting the foundations in place through our HR Consulting Bootcamp Programme.

I also share a link to stories for consultants who have been in business for 5 years and capture their honest insights of their journey – the highs and lows.

There are also practical exercises plus downloadable forms and documents for you to use time and time again. The link to these resources is found at the back of the book and on the relevant pages.

It provides stories and tried and trusted exercises that we use on our workshops and coaching. This book leaves space for personal reflection on each key chapter and a place to jot down your action points. The methods used are to establish a unique pathway to leaping into consulting and setting up your own business. Think of this book as a personal handbook as you embark on this journey. It requires a certain amount of time, effort, and dedication on your part in order to make this happen, but the advice in this book will guide you every step of the way.

I look forward to supporting you as you embark on your HR consulting journey and make the leap!

Sarah Hamilton-Gill

LEAP INTO HR CONSULTING

My Story

LIVING THE DREAM

As I sit on the balcony, the sun casting golden ripples across the Ionian Sea, I take a moment to reflect on the journey that led me here—living my dream in Corfu. A dream that began back in 1981, when, as a wide-eyed 17-year-old, I set foot on this enchanting island for my very first family holiday abroad.

I still remember the rush of excitement as our plane descended, revealing the turquoise waters and sun-drenched beaches below. It felt like stepping into the pages of *Castaway*, the book I was engrossed in at the time. From that moment, Corfu had me under its spell. Year after year, I found myself drawn back, resisting the urge to fully embrace my own Shirley Valentine moment, yet always yearning for more than just a fleeting visit.

At some point, the dream of making Corfu my home shifted from a distant longing to a plan in motion. Advances in technology—particularly cloud computing—meant I could continue running my business seamlessly, even from across the sea. The pieces slowly began falling into place.

In 2019, that long-held dream became reality. I made the move, and the business and I not only survived but thrived. That first summer in Corfu turned out to be one of my busiest, proving that a fulfilling, international lifestyle didn't have to come at the expense of success. In fact, I found myself earning more than many of my former corporate-world colleagues—all while enjoying a life that felt richer in so many ways.

No matter what your dreams are there will be a right time for you to fulfil them – it took me many decades before I was finally in a position for this to happen.

This book will guide you through how you can create a business like this too. So many people tell me they want to travel, or to have the flexibility to move to different locations.

My first piece of advice for you is: don't wait as long as I did !

It's possible sooner than you think. In this book, I will show you how.

MY EARLY STORY

Retail pharmacy

My dad was a second-generation pharmacist and as I was growing up, I was surrounded with aspects of life as the daughter of a business owner. The evenings where he would do the invoicing or order stock were just how it was. I also remember the fun I had going to work with him. At the time, before "just-in-time" deliveries, the business had a large warehouse that stored the stock for the six shops based around Birmingham. I became the delivery driver's helper, the accountant's helper, the stock controller's helper and then the shop worker and dispensary helper – I loved the variety and I think this childhood really cemented my love of wanting to have a business. Initially I was going to take on the business after getting a place at Aston University to study pharmacy, but this all changed as you will hear later.

School life

Switching to my school life for a minute, I remember clearly when I was about 15 my parents coming back from parents' evening at the boarding school I was at in Worcester, and relaying to me the comments of one of the teachers: "The prediction is, Sarah, that you will probably only get one O level." (For those too young to know, an O level was the equivalent to the current GCSEs.)

Whilst I'd never been an academic star at school, I didn't think I was that bad, so I guess it was probably that comment, on the back of a number of others during my schooling, that became really important in terms of driving me to be better than I was and also to prove a point. I didn't want to be the person with one O level. I had plans: I wanted to do my A levels, I wanted to go to university, I wanted to do other things that other people did, and so that one comment from that parents' evening was pretty much engrained in me for many years to come, all the way through the very early parts of my career. I've also had a real passion for self-development. I didn't realise the extent of this until I was being interviewed for a particular role before I went into consulting, and one of the interviewers said, "So what is it that drives you, Sarah, because you are very driven?"

And I reflected on some of the comments that had been made, and really I just didn't believe that I was good enough, so I was trying to prove myself. I got ten O levels, I then got three A levels; okay I didn't get the great grades at A levels but that's another story and entirely my responsibility. I went to university but I didn't do the course I planned to; I was going to do pharmacy and take on the family business that had been in my father's family for two generations but I couldn't do that as I had missed the whole of the summer term during my A levels. With my new lower grades , I had two weeks to decide on what my destination was going to be if I wanted to go to university, and I decided my passion, having been brought up in a family of retail pharmacists, was to do business studies instead.

University life

So I applied through UCAS clearing to get a place at university to do business studies, and given that it was two weeks before the beginning of the new term, nowhere had a space, so I ended up on a hotel and catering degree in Portsmouth, which at the time was just switching from a polytechnic to a university. The way they sold it to me was basically it was the same lectures, the same courses, but on top of that I was only going to probably do a few lectures about food and beverages and various other topics related to the hotel and catering industry, and other than that it would be exactly the same as the business studies. So, there I was, off I went to university, did my degree, got my degree, then did a post-grad in HR management, and throughout my career I've always subconsciously remembered that comment. I've done two master's degrees, and it's fair to say I haven't finished both of them, but I've studied and learnt a lot, and I've done many other courses of self-development. I'm a master practitioner in NLP, I became a qualified complementary therapist and teacher, and I've become a university lecturer, so that one comment was really, really impactful in driving me throughout my career and in terms of my self-improvement. Frightening really, isn't it?

Childhood critics

So what you hear as a child is really important and I'm sure you've probably got some dialogue in your head also that either may be driving you forward or might even be holding you back. It's worth reflecting on what's serving you well and what old beliefs you might have from childhood that you need to revisit and just check out whether they're relevant now, or whether they serve you well. It also took me many years to hear "I'm really proud of you". My partner is proud of me and he has written a message for me on my whiteboard that reminds me of this daily. This was something I was always seeking from my parents; I always wanted them to be proud of what I did, and I'm sure in their own way they were proud of me but very rarely did I ever get any feedback or have it articulated that it was something that they felt. Even when I reflect on this, I still get emotional.

My new cheerleaders

My friends tell me on a regular basis how proud they are of me, and for me that is so important. One of the things you'll learn if you become an HR consultant is that you don't get much feedback. Your clients are paying for your services, they expect you to provide a good service, so therefore sometimes you only ever get feedback if it's negative. However, I would encourage you to always ask for regular feedback, make sure that you understand what a good job that you're actually doing, and if there are things to learn, have plans in place to improve yourself and your business. Feeling good about the work you do is really important, as is entering yourself for awards, and I'll come back to this later.

Boarding school

So that was part of my big story, the "one O level" comment. Another thing that has been central to my life is that as a child at a boarding school (I went to an all-girls boarding school from the ages of 11 to 16) I had very low self-esteem. I never felt I was good enough and could never understand quite why I had been sent to boarding school, and really completely lacked confidence. I was in a boarding school that was like something from the Dickensian period. It wasn't quite like the boarding schools of today where you have your own private rooms with desks, TVs and internet. This was pre all of that and there was a real possibility of bullying, not in the sense that was extreme but in the subtleties, the comments and remarks, so you'd start to question yourself. I think this low self-esteem manifested itself in several ways and in my early teens and early twenties I started to put weight on and then my esteem got even lower. One of the challenges that I had as a consultant for many years was making sure that I looked after my health. I would almost feel sick before events.

Imposter syndrome

One of the reasons I think that I had low self-esteem and confidence was that I never really felt that I was good enough. It's called imposter syndrome and nowadays you can read a lot of information about this topic. It's a very complex subject and not something I can go into in detail here (though I do comment on it more in Chapter 9 – Confidence), but it's certainly something to reflect upon. For me it meant that I doubted myself, that I thought I was never good enough, I thought I'd never done enough research, that maybe somebody would trip me up, maybe somebody else was better than me. All these thoughts can kick in.

My point to you is there are many times where you might face the highs and lows of feeling confident and not confident and having low self-esteem. It is something that you can overcome. The longer you're in consulting the more feedback you get. The more you work in collaboration with partners and colleagues and associates, the more your confidence will grow in terms of what you're doing, and other areas of your low self-esteem can be addressed equally through this profession.

Hurdles

There were a few hurdles that I faced along the way in my career as a consultant that I overcame. Some of them were self-beliefs I had, some of them were situations that I fell into. One of the beliefs I had (and again this stems back to the comment of the teacher and the one O level) was that I never felt I was bright enough for consulting.

Hurdle 1 – Self-belief

I'd got into consulting initially working with somebody that was an Oxbridge student, an extremely bright individual, and again it came back to imposter syndrome. I never thought maybe I was as good as them or that I had enough knowledge, but over the years I've realised that it's not necessarily your academic capability, it's how you apply the knowledge you've got, how you make it come alive for your clients, how you integrate it into their business. And more importantly than anything else, you really do need to understand how businesses tick, the commercials, the financials, what the dynamics of boards are and how you influence people.

Academia is only one element to being intelligent. There are lots of different areas; being emotionally intelligent is important and being able to influence. So, I look back on my thought process of not being too bright, and actually again that's probably been a driver in my life to prove that I am, and now I'm relaxed about it. I know the work I do is good. I have been awarded a Top 30 HR thinker as well as Finalist of SME Business Woman of the Year, so those voices of doubt are no longer there.

Hurdle 2 – Being a single parent

One of the other very large challenges in my life which you may also face or have faced, but hopefully won't, is that early on in my consulting life I became a single parent. I can remember having two very short maternity leaves. I'd had the business for two years when my first son was born just before Christmas. I took off the whole of Christmas and went back to work on January 3rd/4th. My second maternity leave was even harder. At this point I was a single parent and I took two weeks off after a caesarean.

For the next 21 years I then had various challenges in terms of juggling running a business, bringing up two boys who I adored and finding the balance so that I wasn't compromising anybody within that equation. What I did find is that the consulting work gave me some flexibility that I would never have had being employed as an in-house HR professional. Having said that, your clients are very demanding so you can't have total flexibility, but you do have a large amount of control over what you do and when you do it. In terms of the conflicts of work commitments versus supporting your children, I ended up having a team of people supporting me, and I'm not ashamed to say I had an au pair in the house that supported me in looking after the boys when they were very young so I could go out to work and create a future for them.

So if you've had in your mind "I'm a single parent, I need my financial stability, this isn't going to work for me", it can work for you and it did work for me. I'm not saying it's easy but it is very doable and in fact it's a much better solution for you than having the demands and the frustrations of trying to get flexibility when you're in a corporate world.

So please don't let single parenthood become a barrier to you being a successful HR consultant or growing your own business. I had a business that turned over a million pounds a year and I had two very young children.

Hurdle 3 – Health

The third hurdle that I have had to overcome as an HR consultant is my health, which goes back to the previous point probably about being a single parent. Over the years I have never put myself first; it has always been the boys, the business, the clients, everything else, and that's had its impact on me. The only occasions where my business has failed, or has been less successful, is when I have been unwell.

Jamie Oliver

We celebrated our tenth anniversary, in April 2004, at Jamie Oliver's 15 restaurant in London and then I found out I needed an operation. As the eternal optimist with virtually no work absences for 10 years I assumed this would be no worse than having a baby. Into hospital on a Friday, back to work the next week.

I was off work for three months and although I had an MD in place, the business was unsustainable without my input and my drive behind it. On reflection the team that were with me should've had the skills and the capability to drive that business further forward without my involvement but I think once you've had your own business you will understand that the majority of the drive and the energy and the passion will always come from you as the business owner.

I took advice and I ended up liquidating the business. I found it such a hard process. I felt like a failure. All the hard work and ten years of growth. I phoned a well-respected business owner and shared my situation with him. It was so reassuring hearing advice from an objective person. He said "Close your business and phoenix it" (a technical term for starting again). There are clear guidelines around what you can and can't do but I soon learnt what was needed and we phoenixed and started again.

I am sure you can imagine that this was a challenge on many levels, but it also taught me lessons about the strategies in my business and how creating a multi-income approach is essential. This was 2004, though, when the digitisation of businesses was less common.

Look after your health or you will have no wealth!

I would now say looking after yourself is equally as important as all the other people that you're looking after. Without your health you cannot deliver good quality work; you won't have the energy, you won't have the vitality, and you won't have the motivation to do it.

Make time for yourself, be disciplined, put time in your diary, eat a healthy diet and make sure you find time for exercise. I know it's difficult; I've been stuck in the car for eight hours a day driving to and from clients but I've found a model now where I've got this balance of going to the gym and eating healthily, and for the first time in my life I actually feel very healthy, very well and very vital. So please take care of yourself during this journey, and every time you see it slipping a little bit just get yourself back on track again.

> Fall in love with taking care of yourself.

PART 1:
Why you, why now?

"A year from now you may wish you had started today"

Chapter 1:
Why now?

Now professionals, like you, are typically looking for more flexibility and freedom in your life. There have been many challenging world and business events over the last decade and this has created restlessness and many HR professionals feel unappreciated and near burnout. Many people have decided that they want more from their careers and enjoy having more time with their partner and family. Senior professionals are swapping their high profile roles for a simpler more fulfilling life.

One thing I have learnt from over 30 years in consulting is that change is not going to go away – and where we have change we have a demand for HR consulting.

I'm sure you want to take more control over your future, your wealth, the work that you do, when you work, and how you get rewarded for your skills.

THE BUSINESS LANDSCAPE

The latest research from many sources highlights that 99.9% of all private businesses in the UK are SMEs. In Europe, the USA, Canada and Australia there is a similar pattern of businesses.

SMEs are classified in several ways, but it is a business that has less than 250 staff. Between 30 and 75 staff it's unusual to have a dedicated HR function. It might be that they have an in-house person that is doing HR administration, but the level of expertise is typically very transactional. Where you can come in as the external HR consultant is to add value at a strategic level to the managing directors or CEOs of these businesses. Working alongside their administrator you can add value and become a trusted HR partner. The sweet spot for consulting is between 75 and 250 employees. It's at this stage of growth that the systemisation of the business becomes a priority to grow further. And this means all areas of the business, including the HR function.

HR teams are overstretched

Not only are SMEs in need of your services but HR functions in larger organisations are under-resourced and needing to manage the operational issues. The increased volume of new practices and policies means there is little or no room to implement more strategic key projects.

Challenges around remote working, engagement, talent management and moving offices need additional support. The market is forever changing and over the last 3 decades there have been "hot topics" and trends that have driven the demand for consulting services.

There are thousands of businesses that need HR support for them to survive and grow. And it is true that there are hundreds of thousands of HR consultants in the marketplace, particularly in the UK. Many HR consultants fall into consulting without much training, development, or structure.

Mentoring and coaching can accelerate the success of a new consultant and the purpose of this book and our programmes is to ensure that this transition to being a consultant is successful and that income can be created to replace your current salary and beyond. After all, you don't want to be working long hours purely to replace the salary that you've already got. This is about creating a lifestyle and a business that you are passionate about and that give you the flexibility to build your other commitments and passions too, whether it's taking your dog for a walk, picking the children up from school, going to parents' evening, seeing your elderly parents – whatever it is that you would like to do and have more flexibility for.

THE CONSULTING MARKET

Corporate consulting market

According to recent research the UK is the second biggest market in Europe, and this is based on the large consulting firms as the data is not collated for self-employed consultants and small consultancies.

The larger firms are typically involved in multidisciplinary areas for large multinationals and command significantly higher fees than smaller consultancies or consultants.

Independent HR consulting marketplace

I was asked the question recently about the number of people in consulting, so I did a LinkedIn search for HR consultants in the UK and found 164,000. I also then did a Google search for HR consultants in the UK and this brought up 128,000.

I was talking with an HR professional this afternoon and she was worried about the large number of consultants in the UK and that it would be difficult for her to find work.

When you look at the largest client base for new HR consultants it is, as I have mentioned already, likely to be SMEs.

I have added some more research for you below, so you can see the context of the opportunities that exist for you.

The figures speak for themselves

According to a recent article written by Merchant Savvy[1] their research shows that there are over 5.55 million private businesses with fewer than 250 people.

The three busiest regions for SMEs are the South East, South West, and East of England.

Whilst this might have impacted the level of business that was available for HR consultants traditionally, the shift to remote working and virtual meetings has opened up the marketplace beyond the "local" businesses to a national reach. This makes consulting much more viable regardless of where you live. We have consultants from Scotland to the Isle of Wight that now benefit from the technology revolution.

Currently a third of all SMEs are in London, although the move away from corporate head offices in prestigious locations has already started to take place and it will be interesting to see the new figures in a couple of years' time.

All I can say is that there is plenty of work whatever your niche is.

> *And remember, remote HR services open your reach to be national and international and provide an opportunity for you to live where you want to live.*

Now is the right time

I have spoken to many people in recent months about whether now is the right time to go into consulting. Now is absolutely the right time; the business world is full of change and sadly this isn't always all positive. However, where there is change there is also the immediate need for HR support from an operational point of view mainly and also a strategic input. There are going to be significant mergers and acquisitions, there are going to be redundancies, and of course there are going to be those companies that thrive in the next 18 months to two years as well.

Whichever way you look at it, there is going to be a demand for HR services and the key to this is that you're ready and to have your packages, your services and your products clearly defined so that your potential clients know who to reach out to.

Our VUCA[2] world

VUCA is an acronym that has been in use since the late 1980s and is used in consulting and business frequently. As we are in a VUCA world (Volatile, Uncertain, Complex, and Ambiguous) people are searching for that sense of security, purpose and belonging. As a consultant I often hear that people are worried about losing their workplace team and become lonely or isolated working for themselves.

This is why I have grown a number of community groups for my "tribe" – a group of like-minded consultants looking to grow their business and who have similar values of authenticity and a heart-centred approach to work.

Authenticity is becoming more important and when you are your true self, you attract people that align with you and your values. You resonate with others.

When you market to your highly engaged tribe it becomes easier for them to buy from you.

VUCA is just one model of change. If we layer onto this the political, economic, social and environmental changes and all the other uncertainties that are happening in the world right now, change is accelerating at a pace that we've never seen before and as an HR consultant you will need to be ahead of the curve, thinking about what your clients are likely to need as part of their business survival and growth strategy.

Do you want more?

With the many conversations I have every day with consultants and HR professionals like you, these are some of the key areas that are highlighted consistently in terms of what's important and what people don't have enough of right now. I wonder out of the five that I mention below

which ones are important to you too, and maybe there are others. I'd be intrigued to know what they are for you.

Later in the book we will look at your personality and how this will be one of the drivers as to how restless you are in terms of wanting more from your life, and also at the continuous improvement of yourself and your career. Consultants are typically avid learners and like to be continually developing their own skills and knowledge. They are changemakers and influencers.

1. Flexibility

Are you currently reflecting, and feel that there is more to life than what is happening in your world right now? Many people have had a level of flexibility to work from home, and maybe you've always had the advantage of working from home one day a week without going into the office on a daily basis. The trouble is that once you've had this taste of flexibility it's very difficult to go back to the rigid approach that many organisations have in terms of working hours and where you work. The number one reason people decide to set up their businesses for themselves is to create flexibility. You will see this in the statistics later in the chapter.

2. Freedom

Consultants that are setting up have a vision to be able to have the freedom to work and travel around the world. I can relate to this; I had a dream of wanting to live in Corfu for nearly 40 years. I also know that it's not possible to live in Corfu without an income, and given that the majority of work on the island is tourism and travel related and you need to speak Greek or at least be happy to do a lower paid role, it was important for me to wait until I was financially in a position to make this transition.

What made this possible for me was setting up a business that was completely flexible and gave me the freedom to work anywhere in the world. I have always had an interest in cloud-based technology, even when it was newly launched in the late 1990s. All my business systems are cloud based, including finance, the client relationship management system, marketing and HR. With this in mind and if you create the right business structure, it is possible to take your HR consulting business anywhere in the world whilst retaining your clients either in the UK or worldwide if you have a digital presence.

(Cloud technology is where data is stored on servers remotely and not on your local drive. Google Docs is a well-known example, as is Dropbox, and a whole range of SAAS (software-as-a-service) software that we talk about in Chapter 13 – Courage.)

3. *Appreciation*

Another key aspect of you wanting more is about the level of appreciation you get in the HR profession. There have been many recent articles about how HR doesn't get a seat at the board or a voice at a strategic level and on top of this you don't get the regular recognition that you deserve for the work that you contribute to an organisation. Now this isn't true for all organisations but having spoken to many HR professionals over my HR career it is clear to me that there is a huge gap in expectations between the level of appreciation needed and what is actually received.

4. *Wealth*

In terms of motivation, many HR professionals don't go into the consulting industry because they are driven by achieving wealth or high incomes, however there comes a point where the level of effort and input that you give to your career and your company outweighs the level of remuneration that you are receiving. You may be at the point where you think that you would really like to be rewarded more fairly for the effort that you put in. This is a motivator for people wanting to become consultants: earning your income based on the level of effort that you put into your business. We will return to "effort" later.

5. *Control*

Do you want more control in your life? This isn't to say that you are a control freak but there are many things that you would like to have greater control over. You may like to have control over where you work, when you work, what you work on, who you work with, how often you work and also a level of control over your financial stability. Many people have not gone into consulting because they are concerned about the level of risk that is involved in the financial stability of being self-employed. If we reflect on the current business climate it's clear to me that many people have suddenly realised that being in corporate life as an employee is actually not the stable environment that it used to be. From having a sense of stability and low risk, many people have found themselves having little control over their stability, impacting them both professionally and personally. One thing I have noticed with my colleagues in consulting is that there is a greater sense of control over their destiny, providing the right business structure is in place.

Now let's look at some of the research I carried out with CIPD members from a LinkedIn group, to get some answers to the questions I posed.

THE KEY FINDINGS FROM THE CIPD LINKEDIN GROUP SURVEY

The CIPD (the Chartered Institute of Personnel & Development) is the professional body in the UK for HR and people development professionals.

I conducted this research with over 100 CIPD members as to whether they would consider consulting as a career option in the future. Just like you are now.

I gathered a lot of useful information that enabled me to understand my potential clients better. Here I highlight some of the key statistics so that you can see how you might compare to their answers and understand that you are maybe not alone in your thoughts.

The results

I have addressed some of the common questions I am asked and how they map into the results.

Q1: "Have I got enough experience to become a consultant?"

As you will see from the breakdown of those that took part in the survey the majority of the respondents had been in HR more than five years.

I find this particularly interesting and it clearly demonstrates to me that at least 5 years in HR is the minimum before considering consulting but 10 years in HR may be the trigger point. This reinforces the conversations that I have with HR professionals considering consulting. There are a few life events that are likely to take place in your mid-30s to 40s. We have parenting, divorce, children becoming more independent and, dare I say it, age discrimination.

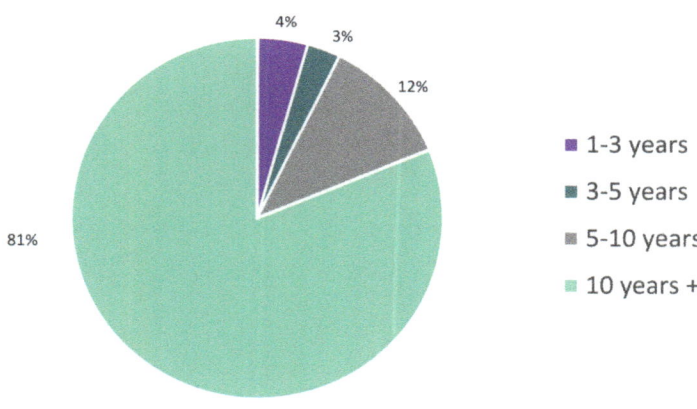

Q2: "Do I need to upgrade my CIPD membership to be a consultant?"

This is the next most common question I am asked. It depends on who your clients are going to be. If you aim to target SME owners, then I am afraid that many MDs won't even know what the CIPD is. This isn't to say it's not important but the priorities as a consultant are different.

The CIPD are working with several independent consulting groups to incorporate the work of HR consultants into the professional development map. This work is still ongoing and we look forward to supporting the CIPD with these initiatives.

So, the answer to the questions about membership is that if you have it it's useful to keep and to maximise the resources available through your membership.

The breakdown of level of membership for the respondents also correlated with the length of time in HR. It was however surprising to see 20 people with an associate membership level.

Do you need to upgrade? Upgrading as a consultant is a lot harder than when you are in corporate life and it's a lengthy process. With my business coaching hat on I would say focus on your business first and when you have spare capacity consider upgrading.

What level of CIPD Membership do you have?

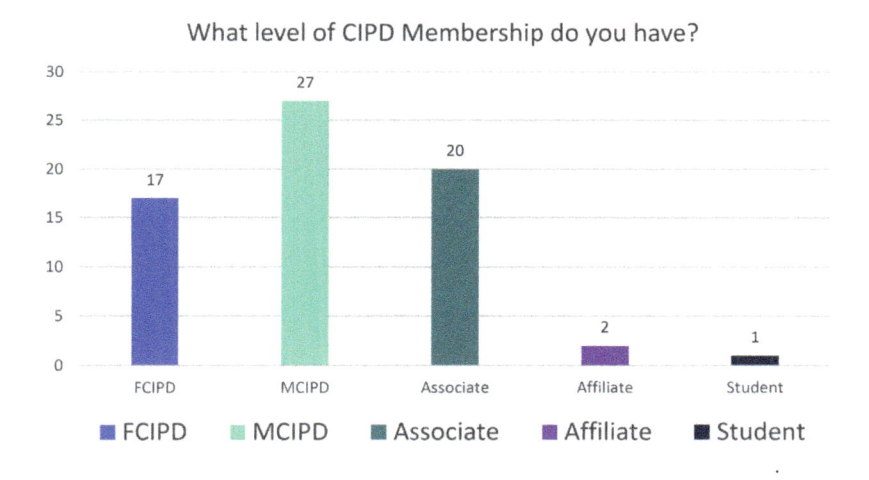

Level	Count
FCIPD	17
MCIPD	27
Associate	20
Affiliate	2
Student	1

If you decide to work with corporate clients where you will be partnering with HR functions, then I would say that this is far more important. However, I do know many consultants that have extremely successful careers without the CIPD qualifications or membership.

Q3: How engaged are HR professionals in corporate life?

Not very by the looks of these responses. If you are engaged in your current role, why would you consider consulting?

84% of those surveyed would consider a career in consulting. That would suggest that there is a serious shortfall in their needs being met in their current role.

If you are reading this book, then you are likely to fall into this category too?

Would you start a career as an Independent Consultant?

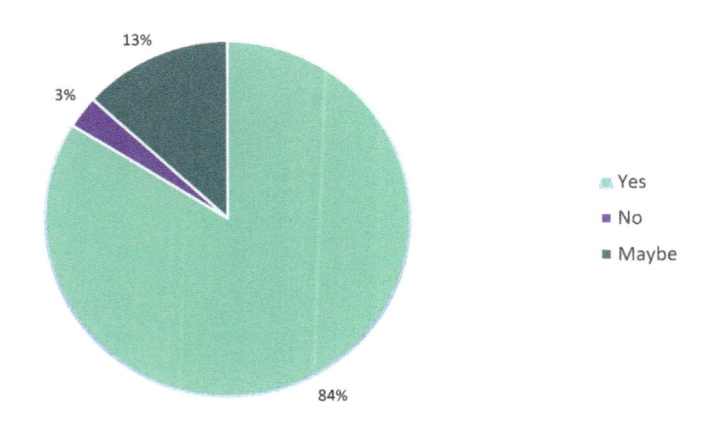

- Yes: 84%
- No: 3%
- Maybe: 13%

It's not always about disengagement at work; it can be your desire to do your own thing. If you have a preference for non-conformity, then this attribute is hard to squash.

Q4: An independent consultant or growing a consultancy?

When people set up business, they rarely start with a plan to grow a consulting business. I was happy working from home with some administration support. Then I moved into a shared office and before I knew it there were 21 staff, a 10-year lease on an office and £1m turnover. Most of this wasn't in my vision.

These statistics below support my belief that it's rare for people to have these aspirations to start with, with only 27% stating they would want to grow a business.

PART 1 || WHY YOU, WHY NOW?

If you went into consulting, would you stay as an independent or would you like to grow a business?

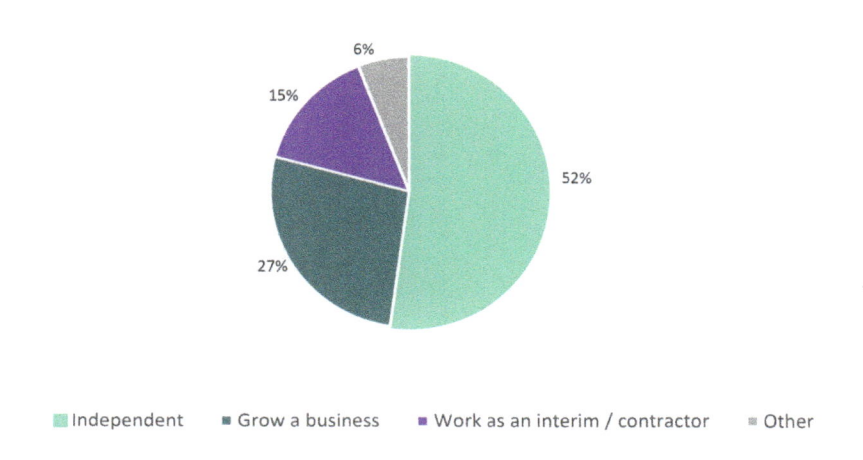

- Independent: 52%
- Grow a business: 27%
- Work as an interim / contractor: 15%
- Other: 6%

Q5: What hours would you like to work?

The number and flexibility of hours are key for people going into consulting. However, be warned, consulting and business success are addictive! So, it is easy to fall into the trap of working long hours again, although this time you are reaping the rewards.

57% of responses are for a desire to be part time or have flexible working. Flexibility is a key factor when I talk to people about setting up in consulting. This along with freedom.

What hours would you like to work?

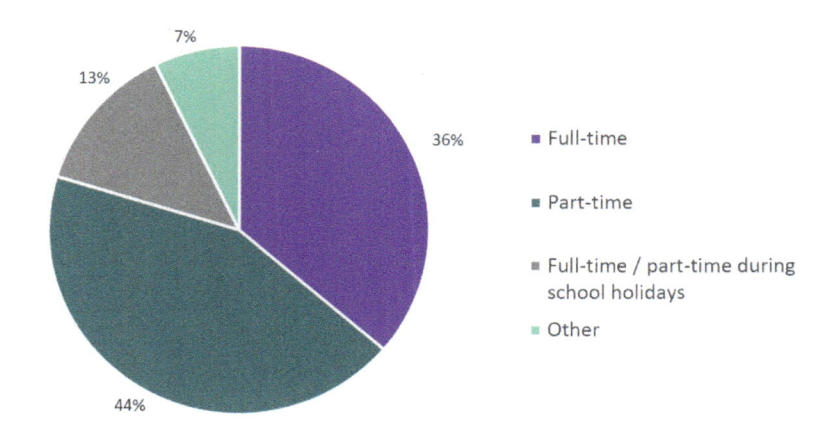

- Full-time: 36%
- Part-time: 44%
- Full-time / part-time during school holidays: 13%
- Other: 7%

Q6: What are the barriers to being an independent consultant?

One of the questions asked was "What stops you dead?"

The four "stop you dead" moments are:

- Cash flow and money to pay bills
- Finance to develop an idea
- Having to do sales and marketing
- Timing in my current situation

Not having colleagues to work with or credibility were not an issue.

Having said this, one of the benefits I hear from people joining our community groups is the sense of belonging and support that this brings to what can be perceived to be a lonely profession.

Here is some feedback that I received from a lady that made the leap earlier this year:

HR Bootcamp – Perfect if you need that final push to follow your dream

"I would absolutely recommend the Virtual HR Bootcamp if you are thinking about setting yourself up as a consultant or you have been going for a while and need to refocus. I was a bit dubious about how much I would get from the course given that I had just had a coaching session with Sarah and had been given LOADS of hints and tips. However, I have met some absolutely fab people who I would like to stay in contact with. I thought being a consultant would be lonely and I wouldn't have much support, but I actually feel more connected and supported by this group than my own current employer."

Q7: Why would you go freelance?

The CIPD members research supports feedback I get all the time.

The key reasons for going into consulting were:

1. Flexibility
2. Do work I love
3. Be my own boss
4. Self-achievement

Numerous polls in LinkedIn reinforce these figures. When asked what the benefits of consulting were, these were the answers:

What are the benefits of moving into consulting?

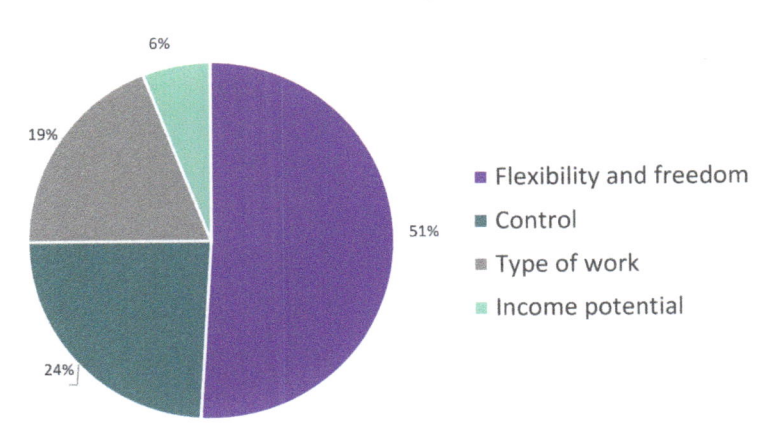

- Flexibility and freedom: 51%
- Control: 24%
- Type of work: 19%
- Income potential: 6%

I wonder whether these factors would change two years into the consulting journey. This is certainly additional research that I will be doing in the future. I hope the research was useful in hearing what your peer group thought and now it's time to turn our attention to you.

Chapter 2:
Why you?

Apart from wanting more, your personality may be steering you towards making this move. In this chapter I explore a number of scenarios that may resonate with you. I also look at some of the drivers behind you considering going into consulting and how you might create a work–life balance that works better for you.

WHAT IS YOUR CURRENT SCENARIO

Scenario 1 – Are you a budding entrepreneur?

Have you always wanted to run your own business? Maybe your parents had their own business, like mine, and inspired you or maybe someone else inspires you to go it alone?

As I have mentioned, I grew up with my father who was a second-generation retail pharmacist with six shops, a warehouse and logistics. I spent most of my school holidays working in the business from a very early age, sometimes helping and at other times creating complete chaos by just being a distraction. By the time I had chosen options at school I had already decided to become a pharmacist and I loved the business side as well. I saw the long hours that my dad put into the business and the passion he had for it. It's a seven day a week business and in those days, you were lucky to get half day Wednesdays and some Sundays off. This still happens in the New Forest but then this is a unique part of the world that sometimes hasn't quite caught up with the new ways of commerce.

On the flip side I also saw the benefits that running your own business can give you. The flexibility to spend time with us as a family, the investment that my parents were able to make in us all going to private schools, and the annual holidays to Devon.

I had a real desire to have my own business and in the early days I always thought this was to become the third generation of pharmacists in the family. I had a place to study pharmacy at Aston University in Birmingham. This all changed abruptly as I discussed in more detail in "My Story".

If you have studied NLP, you will see that this was a "towards" motivational strategy i.e. the carrot. The alternative to a "towards" strategy is an "away from" strategy. This is when you are motivated to do something to get away from something. It is often referred to as the "stick" approach and is a more negative motivator.

Going into consulting for me was a balance between the two. I wanted to have my own business, although at the start of my consulting journey I had only ever aspired to be a successful independent HR consultant. I also wanted to get away from the HR manager roles that seem to constrain me in a world that seemed too slow to get things done and lacked creativity. My HR director once said to me, "Sarah you have lots of ideas, and for every five ideas you have some are OK, one is dreadful, and one is a real gem." These real gems have allowed me to grow and shape my business, changing and evolving to market needs and to create leading edge products.

Every person I have met can create fantastic products and services and no two consultants will have the same background, personality, or experience so there's plenty of room in the market to have your niche.

Over my consulting career I have developed close friendships with many of my clients, MDs, CEOs, and a range of people professionals. If the risk of failure was minimised most of my clients would like to become consultants or business owners. This is one of the reasons why I have written this book and run bootcamps to ensure the successful transition from corporate life into being an independent consultant.

Typically working for someone else will create an income for you, while working for yourself will create wealth and a legacy.

Scenario 2 – Are you a non-conformist?

You may have completed personality profiling throughout your career in HR, or you may have avoided them so far. This may include popular profiles such as the DISC profile, the Five Factor Model or perhaps Myers-Briggs. There are numerous profiling tools that are beneficial for increased self-awareness. I am qualified in a range of them and use them extensively in my consulting work as well as coaching family members and friends!

All these profiles will be invaluable in terms of looking at how you will best suit the world of consulting.

If you have completed these profiles then maybe you have come out as someone that needs freedom (a non-conformist), and to be in control of your own destiny, without the constraints of the corporate world?

Some personalities may suit consulting better, but everyone will have a personal development journey that will never end. I am over 30 years into consulting, and I have already attended three workshops and five online courses this year. This brings me onto the next scenario.

Scenario 3 – Do you love self-development?

As a consultant self-development is essential. Your clients expect you to be up to date and some will expect you to be ahead of the game. Being commercially astute and understanding how businesses work, whatever your specialism is, is critical. If you want to become a strategic partner you need to understand what happens in the boardroom and be able to contribute at that level.

I specialise in HR and leadership development, but I also have a thirst for understanding the bigger picture, both within a company and in the marketplace.

You may become an operationally focused consultant, especially if you are supporting smaller businesses, but the real value you bring longer term will be supporting an MD or CEO to be able to deliver their business strategy.

Being a consultant is a never-ending self-development journey and the beauty is that you can add to your services and diversify as many times as you like. Your self-development will become your key to your future success, keeping ahead of the curve with new products and services, partnering with other associates and companies and providing a team of people you can work with and build long-term relationships with.

Personal Development is: **K**eep
                             Educating
                             Yourself

Remember your personal development is a business expense.

> *"The way we spend our time defines who we are."*
>
> Jonathan Estrin

Scenario 4 – Do you want to have more time for yourself?

Time: we have a limited amount of it, but it is something many of us squander away.

One of the most common issues raised by working professionals is the amount of time that is spent at work and trying to juggle the balance between work and home. I have coached many people and have been coached on this important topic many times during my time as a consultant and business owner. It is very easy to get this balance to be so skewed to work related activities that your relationships and your own health suffer. You may have already recognised that this is one of your key drivers for setting up as an independent and it's good to be clear about how you spend your time currently and how you want to spend your time going forward.

I have given more space to this scenario and topic than some of the others as it's fundamental to your new life.

How do you currently spend your time?

If you were to take a typical week (if there is such a thing), and the circle represents the whole 7 days, 168 hours, what would it look like? Segment your circle to represent the proportion of time you spend in each category. Please add your own categories as well.

Key categories

- Work
- Family
- Health
- Friends
- Commuting
- Housework
- Others

LEAP INTO HR CONSULTING || SARAH HAMILTON-GILL

What does your future ideal week look like?
Key categories

- Work
- Family
- Health
- Friends
- Commuting
- Housework
- Others

Having looked at how you spend your time and how you want to spend it going forward, the next page gives you space to reflect and add action points.

What are the 3 key actions you need to take to move from where you are now to your future you?

Action 1

Action 2

Action 3

What will help you achieve these?

If you now take your ideal future circle, what does this mean to you as a potential consultant?

At the start of your consulting journey the management of your time is essential. As you grow your business and productise your work you will be able to sell more than just your time and the potential of your business will become less dependent on you.

We explore this more in the chapters on Collaboration and Courage, Chapters 12 and 13.

Scenario 5 – Do you have great ideas?

Are you acknowledged as someone that thinks outside the box? When solving problems can you come up with creative solutions?

As I have mentioned before I have ideas all the time, which means I can create new solutions for myself and others easily. This has been with me since childhood. I could do a Carol Vorderman,(a TV presenter renowned for her mathematical genius), and answer a complex maths problem in a new way and get the right answer.

I still have streams of ideas; they never stop. This is one of the reasons I have been nominated and won many awards, including being listed as Top 30 Influential HR Thinker in 2024. It's also why my clients are keen to work with me: they want fresh ideas.

I love the level of creativity I see from new consultants. It's like they have unleashed their inner child with their amazing social media graphics, product ideas and packages.

Scenario 6 – Do you love complexity and challenges?

However, if you want to be an HR consultant working on highly complex problems and solutions, then a high attention to detail and excellent critical thinking and structure will be essential. If you are focusing on transactional employee relations work then consistency will be the key here rather than lots of creativity. Be creative when you are setting up your processes and how you operate but structure and delivering on time will be more important to your client.

Make the best use of cloud technology if one of your ambitions is to have total flexibility on how and where you work. Invest in a great laptop that you can be proud of taking to a client. I once had an IT manager take one look at my laptop (which I thought was pretty good), and recommend that I upgrade it. He made assumptions about my level of success based on the quality of my laptop! We live in a world where first impressions count.

Scenario 7 – Would you love to work with SMEs?

Many potential consultants are attracted to working with business owners and being part of a meaningful business where you can make a real impact.

Many small businesses need support with contracts of employment, staff handbooks and policies so this is certainly an option for many people entering consulting. However, you may well have moved on from the operational work in your role and have spent many years at a strategic level and the thought of "going back" to this type of work may send a shiver down your spine.

Wherever you are now in your HR career you can move your knowledge and skills across to consulting. I have worked with many independent HR consultants that lack the confidence to work strategically to start with. It's your business and your choice where you focus, and part of the equation may be that you must consider the financial aspects as you start up your business. The clients you have and attract when you begin will be very different throughout your consulting journey. I started off offering services to small businesses on a very operational basis. This evolved into a guide for MDs on HR (before googling and the internet existed), with templates and how-to guides.

I found that the micro and small businesses often were very time consuming and much of my time was spent persuading and educating MDs and owner managers on the benefits of HR, or what HR was or meant. With the growth of professional organisations and peer group mentoring I would hope that this is no longer the case.

Scenario 8 – Would you still love to work with larger organisations?

At the start this wasn't within my comfort zone and as the years ticked by and my client base changed, I started to work with large organisations delivering substantial projects at a senior level. I was assessing leadership potential across some of the most well-known international plcs across the UK and running teambuilding events for senior teams. I was once told when discussing a potential team event that the last person didn't work out, so what would I do differently? Given that the "last person" had a very high global profile and huge media presence this made me extremely nervous. What on earth could I do that was better than him?

After nine team building events for the MD and all his teams, I eventually knew I had a winning formula and realised that fame didn't always equate to excellence.

Public v private sector?

Another question you may have is whether to focus on the private or public sector. Again, most new consultants need to build up a client base and credibility in the private sector first and be in a sound financial position. The tendering processes for public sector tenders are long, very detailed and involve demonstrating that you have in place many policies and insurance and you must meet their strict criteria. This involves being a limited company, often having ISO accreditation and demonstrating several years' profitable trading history. Rarely do you get feedback on your tender and whilst the opportunities can often be larger and longer term you will be competing with much larger organisations.

This said, once you have a record of accomplishment in the public sector you will get referred on to other opportunities. I spent many years working with district councils, the Employment Service and the Welsh Assembly Government.

When you set up your business you need to think about the long game and build solid foundations that will allow you to scale the business for success, if this is in your plan.

Scenario 9 – Do you need more flexibility in your life?

There are many reasons why you may need to have this level of flexibility. Many people move because their partners get promoted both within the Forces and in the private sector. For many this may mean not being able to continue with their own career or putting their career on hold. Creating a business with locational flexibility is very possible with today's technology and the move to working from home (WFH) or hybrid working, popularised in 2020.

It has opened thinking around transitioning from corporate to consulting. Homes with purpose-built offices are now seeing a surge in demand by estate agents. Some corporates are also using this as an opportunity to scale back their corporate real estate in expensive city centre locations. This is win–win for employees and employers as long as there are strategies in place for creating engagement and social interaction.

Prehistoric times
When I first started the business in 1994 it was the year that the internet has just been invented, mobiles were like military field kit and no laptops existed. By today's standards it was prehistoric. It did however teach you to be organised in a different way. The distractions of mobile phone, social media and the internet didn't exist.

It meant that you had to be more organised. If you wanted to research something you would have to go to the library, subscribe to a journal or buy a book. There was no Siri, Alexa or Google.

It was difficult to have a high degree of flexibility then. The internet was connected through a cable that you had to dial up to get connected! Only one step up from visiting the Greek Islands in the early 1980s.

When I worked in Corfu in 1982, I made a weekly call home by queueing to get a telephone line from the public box. There were only a very small number of lines off the island and it would take over an hour to get your go. Even then it wasn't guaranteed – and the question of how long you could keep retrying without feeling awkward about how the queue was growing, always entered my head.

Cloud technology

As I have mentioned before, now I run my business using only cloud technology. All my business systems connect, and I can work from anywhere in the world that has a mobile signal or internet.

If you want this level of flexibility you will of course need to define your services around the expectation that your face-to-face time will be limited or via Skype, Zoom or some other platform.

I have dialled into an international conference from a yacht in the Ionian Sea (whilst on holiday), interviewed candidates via Zoom (before it was trendy), and advised on employee relations matters and drafted policies whilst travelling in a VW T5 through Europe. I have sat on our balcony overlooking the turquoise water writing training materials, staff handbooks and many other pieces of work.

Communication is key though to this style of working, and setting expectations with clients is essential, especially if you are working in a different time zone. I love my two hours in advance in Greece. I wake up at my own pace, usually around 8.30–9am and I am still an "early bird" for those waking up in the UK.

In Chapter 13 – Courage I share some systems we recommend for accounting, CRM and marketing. All are aimed at start-ups and are amazing at allowing you to be efficient and create team and project working.

Scenario 10 – Are you struggling to get a "proper job"?

There are unexpected changes that may occur in your life and sometimes this can lead to a period of unemployment whilst seeking out new opportunities. In the meantime, whilst you are looking for a "proper job" you can do some freelance work.

I know several HR professionals that have fallen into this trap and there are a few points about this:

Consulting is a "proper job" and you can't be half hearted about being self-employed unless you don't need to earn money.

Anyone that is self-employed will tell you that it can be a bit like being on a rollercoaster. Highs, lows, and no consistency. The highs are great but bring the challenge of delivering client work when you are stretched to the limit. (This is where your associate pool is very important.) The lows normally follow the highs because you haven't made time to spend on business development and so there will be a cashflow gap.

Consistency of income is essential if you are to keep your health and sanity and with the ability of social media and product development this is now easier to achieve than ever before.

If you know you are going to be busy you can plan your posts in advance and schedule them through several apps and programmes. One is Hootsuite. This maintains a presence but doesn't replace posting insights in real time.

You can also productise your ideas and sell them; you can publish books and e-books and selling on the internet has a global reach. Having multiple streams of income is vital. Why? Because it takes the pressure off you as the sole source of income generation. I recommend that your products, referrals, and other income streams cover your fixed expenses each month.

If you have fallen into consulting almost by accident be honest with yourself as to whether this is right for you and your career. If you are unsure as to whether you have the right personality and drive, look at the further details on https://leap-into-consulting.mykajabi.com/is-consulting-for-you

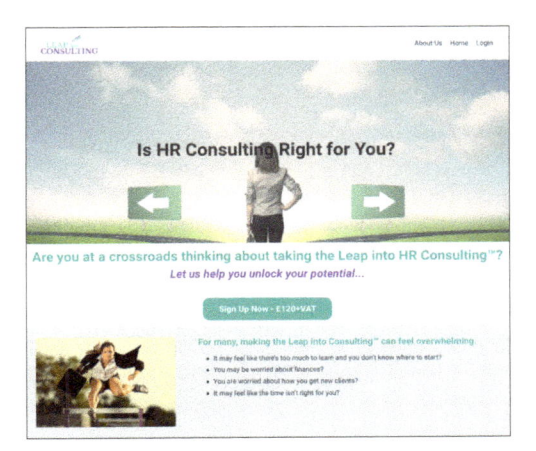

Playing to your strengths will ensure you are passionate about what you do and ultimately why would your client buy something from you if you are not passionate about what you do?

You will find more on this in Chapter 9 – Confidence.

Scenario 11 – Would you rather work as an associate?

There is a vast group of independent consultants that have recognised that business development isn't something they either enjoy or want to do. There is a demand for associates that want to be part of a larger consultancy and to focus purely on the delivery of services. These associate agreements can be on an ad hoc basis or may be a fixed term contract to deliver a project.

This is a great starting point for you if you want to take some of the risk away from being completely independent. Over time this may be ideal for you or maybe you will find that your confidence and skills develop to the point you want to break free. Other consultants I know keep a balance of the two although some consultancies have exclusivity clauses in the contracts to stop this happening.

The best way to accelerate building new partnerships is to attend relevant trade exhibitions, the CIPD in the UK or any other relevant exhibitions. Treat it as being as important as a job interview, look the part, take your business cards and then network and talk to the various exhibitors about associate opportunities.

As an exhibitor it can be frustrating when this happens though, as we are there to connect with our potential clients, and have paid a lot for the privilege of exhibiting to them. Be mindful of this; it is easy to connect prior to the event and just touch base with a card and then follow up within the week. Use LinkedIn and other social media platforms to connect; it's easier and more direct.

We talk more about collaborations in Chapter 12.

Create your consulting business so that you never want another "proper job"

Once you have set up your business and created a plan and start to see how rewarding consulting is, I hope you will never want to get a "proper job" again!

And by the way those that say that consulting isn't a proper job are either jealous or don't understand the world of consulting.

What motivates you to move into consulting?

NLP language patterns help us to understand that there are times when we are inspired by our ambitions and we have a strong desire to move towards our objective. On other occasions we feel more driven to move away from a difficult situation rather than towards a goal.

Reflecting on your desire/need to move into consulting, what is driving you?

What difficulties are you moving away from?

_____
_____
_____
_____
_____
_____

What inspires you to want to create your life as a consultant?

_____
_____
_____
_____
_____
_____

So how can you start to make the transition to consulting? In the next chapter we look at your story and how you can transfer the skills, knowledge and experience that you have into your consulting business.

Chapter 3:
Your future story

In this chapter I share with you how your future consulting career might look in the early stages and how to create a life that maximises your knowledge and creativity and delivers on your dreams. No two journeys are the same, however there are some common themes that appear for many.

So, you've probably been in people development and solutions for quite a while now and you may wonder whether your knowledge and experience is transferable into the world of consulting. You know more than you think and the work and the projects that you've been delivering as an internal head office function would be more than transferable into the world of SMEs and other organisations.

Being a consultant that stands out with a niche is crucial, and you will need to have a blend of commercial ability and technical knowledge. Think about some of the projects that you've been implementing recently:

- What tangible projects have you delivered?
- What were the outcomes you achieved?
- What did you learn from these projects?
- What work have you been involved in which could be turned into a product or service?
- What type of work are you passionate about? That's important as well.

There are lots of HR consultants out there, and you may be asking yourself "How am I going to stand out? How am I going to be different to everybody else?" The key really is for you to be doing what you're good at to start with, be passionate about it, build your client base and then from there you can diversify into other areas and learn more from other collaborations and partnerships you're working with. The key is to maximise your knowledge and be creative, come up with new ways of delivering people solutions, and break the boundaries. Be you, the new you.

BE PAID FOR THE EXPERTISE THAT YOU ALREADY HAVE

The whole environment for HR consulting has changed dramatically over the last 30 years. When I first joined the world of consulting it was quite unique to become a consultant. There were the big consulting firms and then there were a small number of boutique consulting companies that existed.

The world of work has changed considerably; we've heard in the press over the last 12 months about the growth of the gig economy, with 1 in 10 adults in the UK now working this way. Gig working includes using apps to find and deliver work, so our whole world of work has changed significantly. There are a lot more people who have become independent consultants; there's a whole marketplace around interim consulting and contracting and therefore standing out as a consultant and working out actually how you're going to get paid for your expertise has become a little bit more complex.

The big four

Many years ago (and I think some of the big four still do this now), you would probably be able to charge over £2000 a day for your expertise, but equally you can see that we've got social media and various sites now like Fiverr and Bark where you'll find many HR people charging around £45 an hour. Anywhere between those two rates is where you need to decide what your skills and expertise are worth and how they fit into the marketplace you're looking to provide services to.

Monthly salary v day rates

If you're coming from the corporate world or an SME where you're an HR manager or director you're used to being paid on a monthly basis with a fixed salary, and possibly a bonus if you're lucky, with very rarely any overtime or extras on top of that. When you change from that environment to having your own business you suddenly find out that you need to have a day rate or a project rate for what you're doing. This relies on you being able to estimate very clearly how long projects are going to take you, the resources and the expertise that you might need, so there's a whole range of factors that have to be considered when you work out what your day rate is or what your project rate is. Over time you will find out what works for you, what works for the market that you're targeting and also the level of financial success that you're wanting to achieve by becoming a consultant or growing your own consulting business. Read more on this in Chapter 10 – Clarity.

I now specialise in the SME marketplace, but previously I've worked within the public sector and the corporate world. Most of my SME clients want to work with an HR consultant that obviously has the expertise at an operational level or a strategic level, and they're looking for you to provide a return on investment (ROI).

Unfortunately, many of the HR professionals that I've worked with over the last 3 decades don't have a very strong commercial or financial background. The transition into consulting can be quite challenging when you haven't got this mindset. Rather than delivering an internal project which has its issues and complications, you now have to put a business case together, put a proposal together and actually persuade somebody that the work you're doing is going to benefit themselves as the MD, their staff and their organisation.

It's really crucial that you work out from an early stage what your financial position is, what you want to earn, how big you want to grow your business and what you're going to be charging for your services. This will of course change.

Give yourself control over your financial stability

During my years of talking to people in HR I've heard people say, "I'd love to become a consultant but I can't do it because financially it's too much of a high risk, I've got a family, I need to work, I need the stability, I need to know that what I'm getting every month in the bank is going to be the same", and I've challenged people with this mindset on many occasions.

When you're in employment you do have a level of stability, however whatever your input to the organisation you will get a fixed amount at the end of every month. It's very consistent; you know what date it's going into your bank and that helps you plan. But it's rare to have performance related pay in the HR function.

It is a myth however in the current marketplace that you'll get more stability by being employed than being self-employed and I'm not saying it's a bed of roses being self-employed or having your own business but you do have control over the level of income you have, when you get paid and what wealth creation you're going to have. You'll probably ask yourself the question, "Well how am I going to pay the bills in the first few months? I don't know anything about finance so how am I going to manage invoicing and cash flows?"

All these things are very easy to overcome. Look on our book site https://leap-into-consulting.mykajabi.com/Book-Downloads (scan the QR code for direct access) to find some downloadable materials there that will help you. Taking control of your financial stability is good for you, it's good for your family and it's good long term.

Transitioning

The key transition will be moving from your employed status into self-employed or having your own limited business and it's important to balance this exit from where you are now into your new world. One of the fears I hear from potential consultants is that they're not very good at business development or they don't really know where to start with all of this. Again, this is something that is very easy to clarify. My experience over the years is that unless there's an emergency or immediate business problem that needs resolving it probably takes you 3–6 months to build up a pipeline of client work, and after you've won your clients the key thing is obviously to retain them, to offer them additional services and to keep in contact with them. Nurture, nurture, nurture! I talk about this in more detail throughout the rest of the book.

Farming v hunting

I'm very mindful that a lot of my time has been spent developing new client relationships (hunting), often at the expense of forgetting the ones who perhaps haven't got a current project or who are my loyal clients (farming) because I'm very busy as a business owner.

You can't spot opportunities with your clients if you don't understand what is happening in their business.

As above when I made the point about working out what your financials are, it is really important in this ever-changing economy where very large organisations are closing down and the public sector is still short of funding, to take back your control over your finances, your life and creating something that's bigger than a monthly income. It's about investing in your future as an individual and as a business.

CREATING A BETTER WORK-LIFE BALANCE

One of the key reasons that people go into being an independent consultant or setting up their own consultancy firm is that they would like to have a much better work-life balance. They're fed up of commuting long distances, having numerous locations that they need to go to on a regular basis, potentially international travel, they're late home at night, there's then the ongoing 24 hours of email catch-ups, telephone calls, basically not switching off at all. I'm not saying that this will 100% change when you have your own business but you're far more in control in terms of when you work and how you work.

Start-up phase

When you first set out in your business you'll be in this start-up phase. It will be very busy and there will be long hours. It's undeniable, however, that once you've got your processes in place, your methodologies and some of your new clients on board, you can then make sure that you're retaining the boundaries you need to set yourself when you first go into consulting.

Creating efficiencies

One of the mistakes I made when I first set up my first business was that I didn't have enough systems and processes. I always used to pride myself as a business owner for offering a completely bespoke service to my clients, which they loved, because everything was developed almost from scratch.

This is fantastic for your client, but it's not fantastic for you because you're constantly creating new ways of delivering projects which is in essence extremely time consuming and your clients are unlikely to be paying for that extra development time. Systemising what you do and making sure that you create templates, defined products and services makes it clear for your clients and it's also very efficient in terms of your time.

Blended life v work-life balance

The new way of looking at work-life balance is to have a blended approach. Often I'm travelling, but I also spend time in Corfu which is where I live; I often work at different times of the day but I'm available for my clients and most of them don't actually know I'm out of the country. I may work in the evening because that suits me, that's who I am. I prefer working at night.

So, what you need to do is work to your strengths; work when you're really at your best. You've got clients who have expectations about contact and communication but do make the most of what works for you in terms of your energy and your home situation. You may have children, commitments with other businesses or parents, but find a balance that works for you. One of the mistakes I've made over the years is constantly being available for my clients even outside of normal working hours. I must add here that there are no normal working hours when you're in consulting, and most of the clients I have are more than happy to phone me after "normal hours" and occasionally at weekends.

How good are you at setting your boundaries and guarding them?

Now my hours work for me, but they may not work for me in the future. You need to be clear and set expectations and stick to them. This is one of the first areas to clarify with your client when you are scoping out the project. It's a lot more difficult to add boundaries three or four years into the client relationship. The great news is that you will be able to identify quickly which clients are likely to push the boundaries of reasonableness. Being astute during the business development process will give you plenty of clues to how your client makes decisions, their communication style, and their way of working.

This blended approach to work life will help you deliver the best and be at your best more than you would by staying in a 9-5 routine.

Chapter 4:
What is consulting?

By now you may be wondering, what actually is consulting?

Consulting is the provision of services to a third party utilising your expertise on a matter in exchange for a fee. Yes, even when you are a start-up you need to charge for your services! For the consultant, taking an independent and unbiased stance on an issue is central to their role. A consultant can, in principle, service any sector.

WHY USE CONSULTANTS?

Some of the main reasons why consultants are hired are:

- Because there is an unpopular piece of work to be done that is better outsourced e.g. redundancies, restructuring, disciplinaries
- To help facilitate meetings and teams where there are team issues that need resolving or exploring
- To bring fresh, innovative ideas to challenges that face the organisation
- To provide expertise that doesn't exist in-house e.g. assessment centre design

THE PERCEPTION OF A CONSULTANT

You may well have experienced consultants coming into your organisation. Sometimes the perception is that consultants only tell you what you already know and then charge you for it. There are plenty of jokes about this for those that like to poke fun at the consulting industry.

Equally there can be resentment to consultants coming into an organisation, as the sponsor for the programme or the project often listens to and takes on board the suggestions of the consultant when in fact the in-house HR team has been saying these things all along.

Trusted partner

It's highly frustrating for the internal HR function, however as you move into the role of a consultant you will understand how critical it is that the MDs of SMEs have an external partner to be able to discuss confidential matters with. Many of my clients have shared confidential issues regarding not only their business but their personal lives that they would not be able to divulge to anybody. I have been a listening ear to some of the most challenging life hurdles. This has however enabled me to provide the right support for them individually to flourish, and to enable their business to grow too.

I'm sure you can relate to this type of relationship and will value these partnerships in your own business going forward.

Consultants are typically well educated and professional, commanding a presence and with the ability to influence. Many are engaged to deliver change within an organisation where they may not have the expertise or the capacity to do this themselves.

OUTSOURCED STRATEGIC PROJECTS

I have worked with many organisations where they have outsourced projects so that they can continue to focus on their operational HR matters. This has been a blend of both learning and development projects as well as the more traditional HR projects. One of my largest projects was the assessment of senior leadership talent in a telecoms company. It was a complex project with a team of my consultants involved. The project was pivotal in the identification of what excellence looked like, then measuring leaders against the agreed model. This involved development centres, 360-degree feedback and profiling as well as line management assessments. Sitting with one of the most senior people in industry discussing talent in a new way was both humbling and created profound insights.

VARIETY IS THE SPICE OF LIFE

I have provided solutions to over 700 organisations from start-ups to global organisations and in most sectors from obscure projects in nuclear power to mobile telecoms (before it was popular), yacht specialists and the Welsh Assembly Government.

Each project is different, each client is different, yet many of the challenges and "pain points" are similar.

Whatever sector you have worked in to date, this does not mean that is what you will do going forward. I was speaking today to a highly experienced consultant from a large consulting firm who was concerned about how to make the transition into a sector he hadn't worked in before.

My background was retail before consulting, and I have only done a handful of projects in this sector since. I am truly grateful for my experience in multi-site retail as it accelerated my ability to handle the variety and complexity of high-volume employee relations issues. With over 1000 stores under my wing at one point, it soon made me become a SMARTer worker. And these were in the days pre internet, mobile and PCs!

You may have considered joining a large consulting firm. All this would do is transfer you to another corporate – with all the issues you wanted to get away from. Consulting firms are very driven to deliver results for their clients and it's a fiercely competitive marketplace.

On the other hand, independent consulting is what you make of it. The structure you can create for yourself, unlike the top consulting firms where there is a hierarchical structure and "set pieces". You will be in the driving seat.

At this point you may be wondering whether consulting is for you and this is what we explore in more detail in the next chapter.

Chapter 5:
Is consulting right for you?

CONSULTING ISN'T FOR EVERYONE

You've probably built your career in HR on the back of being a technical expert. You've got a good employment law background, you understand employee relations, you're very good at transactional HR. If you've been in your career longer than this you've probably been a good HR business partner and then moved into more strategic HR positions looking at the business as a whole, looking at the strategic direction of the business and having an HR strategy that might go with that. Overall, though, you've been valued for your technical HR expertise within that organisation. You're probably not valued at this stage for your ability to be an entrepreneur or even to contribute at board level, but that's obviously not the case for everybody.

Consulting isn't for everybody, but there are many different types of consulting, so it all depends on what your personality is and what your aspirations are in terms of what you want to be as a consultant.

Your aspirations

Do you aspire to be a fantastic entrepreneur that grows a consulting firm with lots of consultants, staff, associates, and collaborations? Or are you keen to move out of corporate HR, and you'd like to do independent work or become an interim? It's important to understand what type of work it is that you'll be planning to do to start with. This may of course change in time, but at the starting point it is very important to consider this.

Nowadays there are lots of supporting software packages that certainly can help you run your business and if you visit https://leap-into-consulting.mykajabi.com/is-consulting-for-you you'll be able to see some of the forms and even some of the guidance that you might need to decide what type of consulting is good for you.

I have already mentioned profiling and I reiterate that it is important to understand your work preferences before you embark on your journey into consulting.

It's a really good starting point to be able to explore or build on what your strengths are and to look at what are the potential areas that may cause you frustrations or create barriers in terms of your success as a consultant. We're going to look at this in more detail in the next part of this chapter. So how much of your time do you think you'll be spending as a business owner versus how much time as an HR specialist delivering your projects?

I think many people that have gone into consulting (myself included) went into it purely because we loved HR. We didn't go into it initially to set up a business or to employ people, so it's useful to be aware of your development needs to be successful as a consultant or business owner.

Prior to consulting I had never managed a team, and then 8 years in we had over 15 people in my team.

WHAT IS THE BEST PROFILE FOR A CONSULTANT?

This is a question asked time and time again. There are attributes that will make it easier as a consultant and there are attributes that may hold you back.

Take some time to answer these questions.

- Are you highly driven?
- Do you enjoy challenges?
- Do you like the status that goes with your role?
- Do you avoid conflict?
- Are you assertive?
- Do you like networking?
- Can you build rapport quickly?
- Are you able to influence?
- Are you socially confident?
- Are you able to work at speed?
- Do you get impatient for others that are slow to respond?
- Do you like to work at a steady pace?
- Do you like to build relationships with others?
- Do you have a high attention to detail?
- Do you find it easy to come up with new ideas?

This is just a snapshot of some of the aspects that may support or create challenges for you. If you have answered yes to most of these questions then you are heading in the right direction.

Self-reflection questionnaire

As part of one of our short courses "Is Consulting Right for You?" we offer the opportunity to complete a detailed questionnaire along with profiling.

The questionnaire was developed by myself after reflecting on my consulting skills as well as observing many other colleagues and associates. I have specialised in developing behavioural frameworks for a range of recruitment and development projects.

In addition to the questionnaire I have also just launched a new 360-degree feedback especially designed for consultants to get an in-depth review of their consulting skills from clients, peers, team, associates, and partners.

The in-depth self-reflection questionnaire covers these areas:

- Motivational drivers
- Consulting competencies
- DISC profile
- Your approach to selling
- Your attitude to risk and stability
- Your financial safety net
- Your approach to learning
- Professional membership

If you would like to join the mini course you can go to https://leap-into-consulting.mykajabi.com/products/is-consulting-right-for-you. It takes a few hours to complete and involves informative videos and guidance on how to develop each key area.

PART 1 || WHY YOU, WHY NOW?

https://leap-into-consulting.mykajabi.com/is-consulting-for-you

WHAT IS ESSENTIAL FOR SUCCESS?

I'm going to address this one straight away as we have touched on it already in earlier chapters: the whole question about CIPD qualifications.

Qualifications and professional membership

These are some of the most common questions I get asked:

- Do I need to be CIPD qualified?
- Do I need to upgrade to CIPD level 7?
- Do I need to upgrade to FCIPD?
- Should I do a consulting degree?

As I have said earlier there are many reasons to consider all of these options and there are many benefits that come with upgrading and being a member, but trust me, if you are working in the SME space your clients won't even know what the CIPD is, let alone ask what level membership you have. They will judge you on the interpersonal skills you have and how you can solve their problems, without charging a fortune.

I know lots of consultants that have no formal HR qualifications. These qualifications, however, are essential if you are joining a large consulting firm which typically chooses the top universities to recruit from.

Many of the attributes that are needed for success as an HR professional will be useful as a consultant and a number of people have asked me "Is there one particular model for success, are there criteria that you have in terms of what are the essential attributes that might make up a successful consultant?"

I take you back to the point that I made earlier about what kind of HR consultant you are going to be. What are your clients going to look like?

- Are they SMEs, are they corporates?
- What kind of projects are you going to be doing?

Having said that, there are several things that really are quite essential in order to be successful as a consultant, and a lot of these are transferable from what you're currently doing to what you'll be doing in the future. I have outlined these below and through the remainder of the chapter.

Be the expert

First, you'll be positioning yourself as an HR expert so it's important that you know the products and services you sell. You will need to do research. You can keep up to date with best practice and legislation through the various online platforms e.g. CIPD HR-inform. You don't have to know everything, you don't have to be the font of all knowledge, but you do need to have the knowledge that you're saying you've got. Blagging doesn't work especially when you are being paid for expert advice.

If something does go wrong with your advice to a client, which is unlikely, you will have your professional indemnity insurance to protect you and your business. In over 30 years I have not needed to fall back on this policy.

Be objective and challenge the status quo

When you're taken in to a client and you have a piece of work to do, you're often brought in because you're an independent person, somebody that will have the ability to challenge the status quo, and be able to challenge the thinking at a senior level or even at other levels as well. So you need to be confident and have the skills to be able to challenge in a constructive way, offer feedback and facilitate those discussions, whether it's an individual or a team. Building up these skills before you leave employment will stand you in good stead. Please remember though that you don't need to be perfect or skilled in all areas before you leave. You will develop skills very quickly in consulting.

Deliver your projects on time

One of the other essential attributes apart from the ability to challenge and knowing your stuff is that it's critical for you to deliver your projects on time. Very often clients come to you with a specific project that has a deadline by which it needs to be completed. They've probably already got people inside the organisation that frustrate them because of underperformance.

Regardless of the number of other projects you've got in your pipeline, they want to know that their project is going to be delivered, to the right specifications, and on time. Occasionally this means working late at night if the deadlines are tight.

Create and communicate a plan

The more you can do to help them clarify the project milestones and how they're going to achieve it, what your role is and what their role is, the easier it becomes. Which brings me onto the next point about one of the essential attributes for success as a consultant. Communication with clients is very important; they need to feel valued; they need to feel communicated with; they need to know what's happening.

Influence others

Clients don't like surprises and they do expect you to be able to communicate in a way that supports them as individuals. This can be difficult sometimes as you want to be seen as objective but in essence, they are your sponsor and the person that pays your invoices so of course you will be loyal to them. Increasingly an essential attribute of a strategic HR partner is that you need to be able to influence and engage people to make change happen and you need to be able to challenge mindsets and methodologies. You're not in their organisation all the time so when you are there you must be impactful.

Your fears about consulting

If only you could get out of the way of your own success. How many people do I talk to, and I get frustrated because I can see their potential to be a consultant, and they would love to be one, but they are crippled by fear. So, my question to you is what's your fear? What is your real fear about going into consulting?

I will share with you the summary of fears from other CIPD members, but I really don't want you taking these on board as your own fears or seeding doubts that didn't exist before reading this chapter.

One of the questions from the survey that I have already mentioned was:

"What stops people going into consulting, even though they wanted to?" (see Chapter 1 – Why Now?)

Financial stability and sales
Many mentioned financial stability and their fears of having to get work for themselves. I hope that you will see once you have read this book, and joined us on our webinars and Fast Track Bootcamps, that you can overcome both.

Fear of failure
Another fear was the fear of failure: how would that look to their colleagues at their current workplace and to their family and partner? It was about losing face.

Loss of status
Some of the respondents said it was a loss of status; they've currently got this high-profile role, they've got power and status, they've got influence in a large organisation. If these are concerns of yours too, I can reassure you that you will get all these needs met by working with a variety of clients. You will have a greater influence, status, and high profile in the industry.

Support

For some it is a big mindset shift to go from having this larger "corporate" environment where you have support and resources that most small businesses dream of. As an HR professional it's common to have other support functions doing the roles that in a small business you will learn to do yourself. This usually involves IT, finance, sales and marketing. The difference is that your business is a micro business and the support you need to run your business is readily available, often 24/7. The response times are often quicker and the support staff are all highly trained in customer support.

Accountability

One of the other areas of fear is about accountability. There are many people that have a team of people to work with in the bigger corporate environments; they have a team of experts that support them and sometimes (and I'm not saying this is true for everyone, but certainly for some people I've met) you can hide within a team. Your performance can be masked by the sheer enormity of the number of people involved in delivering things.

Being a consultant, you are hugely accountable for your actions, for your delivery. You must take responsibility, and that can be a potential fear for some people.

"I don't have enough experience"

Then of course you get the excuse (and I do call it an excuse):

> "I haven't got enough experience/I haven't got enough knowledge yet … when I've done this, I'll consider it" or "When I've had that promotion…" or "Maybe I just need to do a master's degree", "Maybe I need to do a second master's degree".

It's this fear of "I haven't got enough knowledge or experience", "Who's going to listen to me", all the classic symptoms of imposter syndrome, that is going to hold you back.

If you have been in HR for about five years you've probably had a lot of experience at an operational level, a very transactional level. You've probably dealt with a lot of employee relations issues, and you've got involved in other projects perhaps as a business partner. I would recommend that you start dipping your toe into more strategic work, looking at strategy and policies, change management, values, behaviours, and engagement, all of these key areas.

You may think you haven't got enough experience, but five years' solid experience is fantastic; it's enough to get you started as an HR independent consultant or even to start setting up your own business and working with small-medium size businesses.

Just remember – you know more about HR than many of your clients in the SME marketplace.

Managing director v HR expert?

If someone is running a business with 10 staff, their expertise is whatever they set up that business to do whether it's manufacturing widgets or delivering a service. They're not HR experts. They may be great people managers and great leaders, but they don't have the HR technical knowledge that you have.

So again I say, get out of the way of your own fears and take the next step and really consider moving into consulting because you have the experience and the attributes as I've mentioned before, and you have the desire. You wouldn't be reading this book if you didn't have some desire to go into consulting and to know how to do this.

The 3 Ps

I remember quite a few years ago now, my father standing up at my wedding and in his inimitable way talking about my qualities as a daughter. One of the things he said which has always stuck with me is "Sarah has got this in bucket loads, she has got persistence, and persistence, and persistence." Hence the 3 Ps.

At the time I didn't know whether to be pleased or a little bit offended by his summary of my attributes, however when I reflected on it I realised that actually it is such an important quality to have when you're working in consulting and in life in general.

You will have clients that will delay your project for no reason other than logistical reasons internally or maybe the agenda's changed, or people are off. But your fantastic milestone plan that you made at the beginning of the project may not be stuck to, not because it's your fault, that's just how it happens, and then suddenly you've got four or five clients that are doing the same thing so all of your nicely laid out plans for how you're going to work the next few weeks get juggled, they get changed, they get moved and the implication of this is that your cash flow will probably change because you haven't delivered the work. That's just one example of why you need persistence, and you also need to have influence to make sure that your projects get delivered in a timely way.

Sometimes it feels as if it would just be easier to give up on a particular project when it gets difficult. You might meet a lot of resistance to some of the work you're doing, particularly if you're doing work around change in an organisation. Some people just don't like that. I know in the past I've found it difficult when going through my own change, even if it's been positive. You need to keep on track, be persistent, keep focused and keep going. It's a very important attribute.

The other time when persistence is really important is as you're building your client base. When you start up your business you'll have this possible fear that you're not going to get enough clients, and you're not going to be able to find them ("I hate networking"; "I don't like to talk about money"). So you need to be persistent. If a client says no, it's probably not a no forever; it may be a no just for now. You need to make sure that you put it in your diary to go back to them. Don't take no for an answer; you need to be persistent. You won't grow a business by just walking away every time somebody creates a barrier or a hurdle to your progress or your success.

Resilience

As you're building this increased persistence and influence in your business you also need to consider resilience because you will get knock-backs. There will be times – and I've had them – where you will have to dig deep in terms of being resilient in your life and in your business career.

Resilience is a whole new subject in itself. Visit https://leap-into-consulting.mykajabi.com/products/book-downloads and you'll see some additional resources around how to build your resilience. It's something that starts in childhood and those that haven't ever been put into difficult situations struggle because they haven't had to be resilient, so when they get to later life and face difficult challenges they haven't got that inbuilt attribute of resilience that they need. A key to resilience is how quickly you bounce back when faced with adversity. It's not always going to be easy, but the positive side is that you're building better skills to deal with bigger hurdles and challenges that will come when you develop other programmes for other clients.

It's harder as an independent consultant to get useful and meaningful feedback and so part of the range of development options I have for consultants is the newly developed HR consultant 360-degree feedback questionnaire which is outlined below.

> A SMOOTH SEA NEVER MADE A SKILLED SAILOR.
> — FRANKLIN D. ROOSEVELT

HR CONSULTANT 360-DEGREE FEEDBACK QUESTIONNAIRE

With over 20 years' experience of developing 360-degree feedback software and related products and solutions, as I have already mentioned I have now created a 360-degree feedback questionnaire for HR consultants so that you can gain feedback from your clients, associates, and team. I have outlined the key behavioural competencies here, and additional information on how to complete your own 360 can be found in the resources section at the back of the book.

The behavioural competencies here are based on working with hundreds of clients over a 30-year period and I created the subsequent 32-competency framework to help organisations to quickly understand and articulate the behaviours they need for success.

As with any questionnaire the maximum number of competencies to choose is between 10 to 15.

You may notice that many of these areas are where you can already demonstrate high levels of expertise.

Key behavioural competencies for an HR consultant

1. **Analysis and planning**
   The ability to take in a range of information, think things through logically and plan for the future.

2. **Builds relationships and collaborations**
   The ability to build rapport, work with others and maintain long-term relationships.

3. **Consulting skills**
   A set of skills over and above technical expertise and interpersonal skills.

4. *Decision making and problem solving*
Makes timely, informed decisions that take into account the facts, goals, constraints and risks.

5. *Developing strategic partnerships*
The ability to establish relationships with, and influence, networks of people whose cooperation is needed for the success of your business.

6. *Drive for excellence*
The ability to see where improvements can be made, and the willingness to keep encouraging the change of systems or procedures to achieve those improvements.

7. *Effective communication*
The ability to communicate well and put across your thoughts and ideas through a variety of communication methods.

8. *Emotional resilience*
The ability to take setbacks and difficulties in your stride so that you remain focused on completing what you have to do.

9. *Flexibility and adaptability*
The ability to change and adapt your own behaviour or work procedures when there is a change in the work environment.

10. *Impact and influence*
The ability to make others listen and understand what you are saying and persuade them into following a course of action using both emotional and rational arguments.

11. *Initiative and taking ownership*
Takes on responsibility and accountability for tasks and actions.

12. *Innovation*
The ability to see and create new ways of doing things and find creative solutions to problems.

13. *Self-confidence*
A feeling of self-assurance arising from an understanding of one's own abilities or qualities.

14. *Self-management*
The ability to understand your own motivations and personality and manage them effectively, so that you manage your own time, priorities and resources to achieve goals.

15. *Technical expertise and professionalism*
The skills, knowledge and experience required to excel in your area of specialism.

These 15 competencies are further broken down into statements and there is the option of adding qualitative feedback to the report as well.

The completed report is a comprehensive analysis of all the feedback broken down by category of respondent.

The questionnaire's aim is twofold:

1. To gain valuable feedback about your consulting capability.
2. It's an opportunity to share and review the findings with your clients and discuss additional work opportunities.

CONSULTING CYCLE AND SKILLS

In additional to the behavioural competencies outlined above there are a number of consulting skills that you may wish to develop over a period of time. The skills you need will be influenced by the type of work you decide to do and the size of the projects you deliver.

The consulting cycle is akin to the employee lifecycle. There is a natural process to follow, like a project planning process.

There are many detailed books about consulting skills, and this is a whole new book I could write, but not yet.

Broadly speaking they fall into the following areas:

Business development and client relationship building

- Finding new clients
- Proposal or bid writing
- Milestone and project planning
- Drafting and agreeing Terms and Conditions

Delivering the project

Diagnostics and analysis
- Research and data collection
- Interviewing people
- Running focus groups
- Conducting surveys
- Developing questionnaires
- Psychometric profiling
- Audits
- Benchmarking and analytics

- Present findings and recommendations to stakeholder
- Identify issues and create solutions

Project implementation
- Implement recommendations to clients
- Influence and lead others
- Communicate with stakeholders
- Invoicing and credit control

Review of project

- Project review with sponsor
- Spotting opportunities for further work
- Using metrics and calculating ROI
- Requesting testimonials and online feedback
- Asking for referrals

In each stage of the cycle above you will be able to see the types of skills that you will need to develop. Creating methodologies and templates are going to speed up your projects and create better efficiencies as well as profit.

As a consultant we can now make full use of AI to support our operations and profitability.

Chapter 6:
The benefits of consulting

In this chapter I share some of the other benefits of being a consultant, apart from flexibility and freedom.

The variety of work that you will enjoy for different clients, different sectors, and projects is a real benefit. I have worked with hundreds of clients all with their uniqueness, from SMEs to multinational organisations. It's an experience that is difficult to replicate in the corporate world. As someone with a low boredom threshold I can safely say I have never found consulting boring – ever!

You will have the ability to learn at an accelerated pace, far exceeding having one role in an organisation. You choose what personal development journey you go on. I specialised in executive coaching, and I didn't need any sign-off or caveats to do this. I researched it, got the funds and then did it.

The types of projects you work on are likely to be more challenging, allowing you to use your creativity to deliver solutions to your client. After all, clients don't bring you in to solve trivia, they bring you in to create step change, however big or small that is. Many SMEs are focused on the operational issues of their business and may have limited time or knowledge in specific areas.

You will create value, maximise growth and improve business performance for your client. Clients generally are more appreciative of your services than when you are an employee. You make an impact on their business and life, and for that they are genuinely grateful.

One of the benefits you have as a consultant is the objectivity you bring to the client. You have no history or company baggage and you don't get involved in the day-to-day politics that so often prevents progress from happening.

Creating a better work–life balance is one of the main advantages of being a consultant. YOU can choose where you work and when you work. I talk about this again in Chapter 13 – Courage.

You will be surprised that as a consultant you get listened to far more than if you are an employee. You are valued more, and you can reach senior decision makers much more easily. They are interested to hear about the work you do with other organisations.

As a consultant you may earn significantly more than your peer group in corporate life. I often remind people who make comments on the fees that I charge that the company charges these fees; it isn't what I get paid. It's important that there is an understanding from your clients that you are running a business. Your client has the benefit of not having to pay your national insurance or other taxes and benefits and has no long-term commitment to you.

You will find your own list of benefits from becoming a consultant, not all work related. Some will surprise you as you may not have contemplated them at the beginning of your journey.

I have recently heard some new consultants say that their relationships at home are much better and that they are able to get out and about and exercise more. Their dogs are happier as well!

For many their morale is higher, and they are happier and more motivated.

PART 1 || WHY YOU, WHY NOW?

So where are you?

What benefits of consulting are most important to you?	On a scale of 1–10 how much do you get this currently?
E.g. flexibility	5

When reflecting on the above exercise how is it making you feel?

Action points

- [x]
- [x]
- [x]
- [x]
- [x]

Chapter 7:
What type of business do you want?

In this chapter we look at the many options that you have when leaving the corporate world. This includes contracting, interim work, being an independent consultant and setting up a consultancy.

I then go on to share some of the growing pains you might experience with your business and more detail of how I grew my business.

An area that needs exploring for whichever option you choose is the legal considerations. The main one here is the difference between a sole trader and a Limited Liability business. There are also other legal entities, but these are the two most common.

DO I NEED TO BE A LTD BUSINESS?

In the UK, as I've already mentioned, the two most popular types of businesses are limited companies (Ltd) and sole traders.

A limited company is a type of business structure that has its own legal identity, separate from its owners (shareholders) and its managers (directors). This remains the case even if it's run by just one person, acting as shareholder and director.

A sole trader is essentially a self-employed person who is the sole owner of their business. It's the simplest business structure in the UK.

In the UK there are twice as many self-employed to Limited businesses, as they are simpler to set up and cheaper to run.

Each type of business has pros and cons so it depends what your plans are for your business and the types of clients you will work with.

To explore more about the legalities of business formation for your region it is best to get advice from an accountant and to read the information on the relevant government website.

The key differences between sole trader and a Limited Company are:

- Taxation of profits
- The liability of the owners
- Accounting practices
- The type of ownership
- The type of insurance that you may need
- Funding options for growth

There is no need to rush into a decision but it is a discussion that you can have at the early stages of thinking about becoming a consultant.

We cover this in depth on our bootcamp with our financial guest speaker.

CONTRACTING

If you are considering being a contractor, you will need to review the latest UK guidance on IR35. In essence IR35 is an HMRC rule that determines whether you should be paying income tax and national insurance as if you are an employee, or outside of IR35 where you are running a legitimate business and are liable for your own tax.

With IR35 creating the need to fulfil the requirements of demonstrating that your business is a business in the true meaning of the definition and not an umbrella company for avoiding income tax, you will need to ensure as a minimum requirement that you have a range of clients directly invoiced by your business.

INTERIM ROLES

Not everyone takes the leap straight into working for themselves; there may be a few variations or pit stops before this happens.

As organisations look at options to create a cost-effective HR service and improve profitability, the demand for interim roles has grown to meet the requirements for short- and long-term positions.

There is a demand for experienced senior HR professionals who enjoy the flexible and challenging aspects of interim and for some this means this is an ideal career option after leaving the corporate world.

Interim executives go into organisations and are expected to make a difference immediately, because of their in-depth experience and seniority. Many are director level appointments.

Interim HR work can be a stepping stone and there is a whole marketplace dedicated to supporting people to find work and thrive in this space. This isn't what I specialise in although I have some colleagues that have had many years of hugely challenging and rewarding interim roles.

The danger with interim work is that you get into a cycle of delivering a contract, finding a contract, delivering more work and so it doesn't help you set up your own business with your own clients. The demands of interim work are high and work–life balance is often compromised.

Here are some of the skills needed to be a great interim professional:

- Ability to learn quickly
- Commercial awareness
- Ability to influence change
- Diplomatic
- Achievement orientated

- Resilient
- Ability to remain detached

You will notice that the skill set for interim is very similar to consulting.

How to get into the market

There are plenty of specialist recruitment agencies and now there are platforms specifically aimed at the interim marketplace. As with all aspects of being an independent you will need to be able to sell yourself, focus on what you bring to the party, what achievements you can demonstrate and how you will make a difference.

The benefits of interim v consulting

Interim has often sounded appealing to me as one of the few frustrations in a consulting role is that you are often dipping in and out of working with your clients and don't always see the result of the work you have done first-hand. Interim allows you to be fully engaged and able to deliver a series of projects in a specified timescale.

Often interims are more highly skilled than the person they are covering for and this too can have its challenges. How do you engage a team quickly when their loyalty is to the previous manager, or your ways of working are very different?

The downside to interim work is that it is as difficult to move into consulting from this as it is from the corporate world. You are likely to be trying to build a client base whilst working full time in your interim role. The pace of interim work means you are unlikely to be able to do both.

HR FRANCHISING AS AN OPTION FOR HR PROFESSIONALS

For HR professionals considering starting their own consultancy business, one option is to join an HR franchise rather than going it alone. This option provides a structured business framework, leveraging an established brand and system. However, there are advantages and disadvantages to consider before deciding.

Additionally, some businesses offer a licence model, which differs from franchising in terms of flexibility, control, and support. This section explores these options and provides a clear comparison to help HR professionals make an informed choice.

Option 1: HR Franchising

An HR franchise allows individuals to operate under an established brand, following proven systems and processes. The franchisee benefits from training, marketing, and operational support in exchange for an upfront investment and ongoing fees.

Advantages of HR Franchising

- **Proven Business Model** – You gain access to a tried-and-tested system, reducing risk compared to starting from scratch.
- **Brand Recognition** – You operate under a reputable name, which can help attract clients more easily.
- **Comprehensive Training & Support** – Franchisors provide initial and ongoing training, covering business development, marketing, and operations.
- **Marketing Assistance** – Many franchises offer national or regional marketing campaigns and materials.
- **Operational Systems** – Access to business tools, software, and methodologies that improve efficiency.

- **Community & Network** – Being part of a larger group means you can connect with other franchisees for support and knowledge-sharing.
- **Territory Protection** – Many HR franchises provide exclusive rights to operate in a specific geographic area.

Disadvantages of HR Franchising
- **Initial Investment & Ongoing Fees** – Franchisees pay an upfront fee and regular royalties, reducing profit margins.
- **Less Control** – The franchisor often stipulates branding, pricing, and service delivery methods, limiting independence.
- **Compliance with Rules** – Franchisees must follow the franchisor's operational guidelines and cannot significantly alter business processes.
- **Limited Personal Branding** – You may not be able to promote yourself under your own brand, which can impact long-term business growth.
- **Contractual Obligations** – Exiting a franchise can be complicated due to contractual agreements.

However, there are some new innovative HR Franchises that exist and so it's an area to explore more fully. We can make introductions for you if you would like to find out more.

Option 2: Going Solo

Starting an independent HR consultancy means building your own brand, setting your own pricing, and developing your own client base. While it offers complete freedom, it also requires a strong business strategy.

Advantages of Going Solo
- **Full Control** – You make all decisions, from branding and pricing to service offerings and business strategy.
- **Keep 100% of Profits** – No ongoing franchise fees or royalties, maximising earnings.

- **Build Your Own Brand** – You can establish your reputation in the market under your own name.
- **Flexibility** – You have complete control over how you work, who you work with, and your long-term goals.
- **No Restrictions** – You can pivot your business, introduce new services, or expand without needing permission.

Disadvantages of Going Solo
- **Higher Risk** – Without a proven system, there's a greater chance of business failure or slow growth.
- **No Immediate Brand Recognition** – You must build trust and credibility from scratch, which can take time.
- **Lack of Support** – Unlike a franchise, you don't have a built-in network or mentorship system.
- **Self-Driven Marketing** – You must handle all branding, advertising, and lead generation on your own.
- **No Operational Blueprint** – You must develop your own business processes, which can be time-consuming and complex.

We set up our HR Consultancy Bootcamp to alleviate these issues as well as The HR Consultancy Academy® which is the natural next step after setting up your consultancy. It is a proactive space to grow your business through development and mentorship.

Licence vs. Franchise: What's the Difference?

Some HR businesses offer a licence model instead of a franchise. While they may seem similar, there are distinct differences.

Feature	Franchise	Licence
Brand Usage	Must operate under the franchisor's brand	Can use the licensor's system but often under own brand
Support & Training	Comprehensive training, marketing, and operational support	Limited support
Control	Franchisor has strict rules and processes	Licensee has more freedom
Ongoing Costs	Franchise fees + royalties (often percentage-based)	Usually, a one-time fee or lower renewal cost
Territory Protection	Often granted an exclusive territory	No territorial exclusivity
Flexibility	Limited (must follow franchise system)	High (can run business independently)

Which One is Right for HR Professionals?
- Choose a franchise if you want structured support, a recognisable brand, and a proven system.
- Choose a licence if you want more flexibility but still want to benefit from existing tools or methodologies.
- Go solo if you want total control but are prepared to build everything from scratch.

Final Thoughts

HR franchising can be a great option for professionals who want to launch a business with lower risk and greater support. However, it does come with limitations in control and ongoing costs.

We have supported over 250 consultants to start up their businesses in the last 5 years and with a 90% success rate of reaching one year still in business this outstrips the usual 10% highlighted in research in the UK.

For those who want more independence but still wish to use an existing system, a licence model might be a better fit.

If complete autonomy is your goal and you're confident in building a brand from the ground up, going solo may be the best choice. Everyone's situation is different and we are happy to discuss the best options with you. How you can do this is in the resources at the end of the book.

INDEPENDENT HR CONSULTANT

The complete Leap into Consulting® means you leave your previous employment/career break etc and you start from scratch and create a thriving business. You are responsible for the marketing, accounts, project planning, sales and delivering the project. This might sound daunting or even grand but that is what you need to master in your first year – quickly.

Getting everything right from Day 1 is not necessary. You can build on your knowledge as you acquire more support, clients, and experience.

This is what happened to me.

I was in a regional HR manager's role at Foster Menswear going through a management buyout (MBO) from Sears plc. The directors from Fosters were going to buy the company from the Sears Group and run it as an independent limited business. Not many people reading this book are likely to know Foster Menswear as it no longer exists. It was a very well-established menswear retailer with safe, slightly old-fashioned clothes and suits. Many lads would get their school trousers from here.

The business brought in consultants to work with the board to relaunch the brand and refresh it. This resulted in a new strategy and direction.

The person heading up this programme was someone I knew from school. As the programme progressed, I had several conversations about consulting and eventually the "dream" I was sold persuaded me to leave corporate life and become self-employed, working as an associate for this now well-known consultancy in Manchester.

It was 1994 and I was 30 years old. My parents were looking on the horizon for me to settle down and have a family and I had at this point got a house in Welwyn Garden City. By all accounts they would describe me as independent and successful. At last!

And then...

The bombshell phone call where I explained to my parents that I had given up all my clear perks of a company car, good salary, discount (not so attractive with menswear), and a career ladder. I had no significant savings, but I was naively excited about a career in consulting.

The first few months were tough. I travelled to Manchester on a regular basis and was severely out of my comfort zone on many occasions. I did discover though that I was pretty good at selling and really enjoyed meeting with potential new clients and being able to work out quickly what their pain points were and how we could help. I worked with some large clients, Vodafone (who were just starting out and still in their small offices in Newbury), the Employment Service, Nokia, Yardley, and many others.

I learnt a lot about the consulting cycle and how to deliver work to a very high standard and worked with some amazing consultants from a variety of backgrounds. Keith Dixon, now an amazing best-selling author living in France, was a role model for behavioural science. His calm approach was much needed in those days. I appreciated his wise head then and during many of our joint projects over the years.

With any consultancy where you decide to become an associate there will always be a sliding scale of fees based on how much business development you are involved in. However, some businesses can provide you with associate work without you doing any selling, as they have larger projects they are working on. I started slowly but built a portfolio of work, experience, and my confidence. That's when I took the next leap into going solo.

It was me, a desk in the spare bedroom, a dial up internet and a very clunky laptop (by today's standards).

Chapter 8:
Delivering larger projects and growing your business

There are many models that are available to you as a consultant when scaling up your business. Again, this will depend on what your vision and plans are and what resources you have to grow your team.

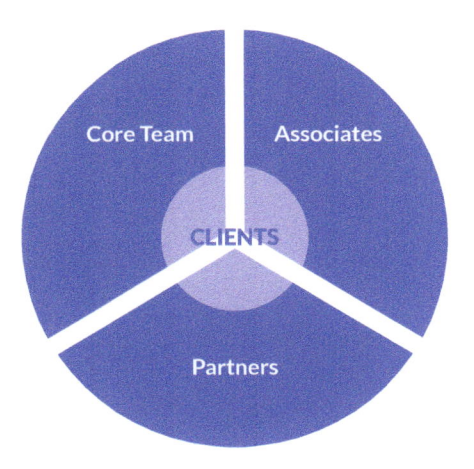

Given the nature of many consultancies that I know, most will keep to a model of a small core team and a range of associates that have unique areas of expertise that can be brought into larger projects.

Resource-hungry events like assessment or development centres often need six consultants, a lead consultant, and a coordinator. In this example the lead consultant is likely to be you, and the coordinator would be a trained member of your team.

The associates would be self-employed or providing services through a limited company and they will understand your values, have a service level agreement with you and have been briefed before the events.

However, to balance the mix of your team they must all be able to represent your business in the way that you want. They are your brand ambassadors. Clients will expect you to have a seamless service whether it is your associate that they communicate with or the support they receive from a product supplier. This takes time and you need good systems to remain joined up. My experience is that your client is unlikely to be interested in the relationship that you have with your team unless it doesn't work well. They want ease of service and a one-stop shop.

KEEP THE END GOAL IN SIGHT

Why are you going into consulting? If you just want to be paid what you earned when you were employed, then you may need to reconsider whether consulting is the best option for you.

However, you may be earning the same amount for less time and more flexibility or you may have your eye on growing a much larger business and great wealth and potentially a legacy.

You may have the dream many business owners have which is to sell their business and run off into the sunset. This sounds idyllic but I have had experience of this and many entrepreneurs I know also struggle once they have sold their businesses (which gave them their focus and identity), unless they have a compelling Plan B.

There is normally a handover period where you are tied in and I know owners that have sold their business, including myself, where the "golden handcuff" is a difficult time. One lady I knew hated it so much she had set a countdown timer on her phone to keep the end goal in sight.

GROWING PAINS

One minute you are worried about not enough work and then before you know it you are worried about how you are going to deliver the work.

You will probably feel stretched to deliver the volume of work and need additional resources. And it's likes buses: you wait for ages and then you get three altogether. Consulting is the same at times.

This is where the questions crop up about whether you need a member of staff to be employed, self-employed or to use freelance platforms such as Fiverr and if you need an office. You don't really want people in your home, especially if you have no dedicated room for them to work with you. Now we are better placed to work remotely, and it has started to become the norm during the pandemic. This opens the opportunity for us as business owners as well as a way of working with our clients too.

The answer is really based on your available funds and the consistency of your income at this stage.

Don't rush into growing!

WORK FROM HOME vs AN OFFICE

Growth hub

My journey from leaving the house was to join a centre where start-ups and micro businesses shared some central services but had private offices. This was ideal: a couple of miles from home and space enough for three desks and a proper telephone system! You laugh but when you suddenly have more than one person in your office you then have the logistics of team working. Handing the phone across from one person to the next with your hand over the speaker isn't the way forward.

There are great VoIP (voice over the internet) systems available now that reduce the costs for micro businesses and it also means that you can "plug in" anywhere in the world using the same number.

Shared offices are also great for motivation and working with other like-minded people. Some centres have introductory offers and the notice periods are much shorter now than they used to be (usually 1–3 months' notice). If you are worried about the image of your office or where you are you don't need to be as 95% of all your clients will never visit you. It's your office so stamp your personality on it and make it an environment that works for you and your new team.

The office in the UK

Our UK office is in a tranquil log cabin, with three desks and a small meeting room. We open the doors in the summer looking out onto a pretty cottage garden. We have the office cat Dexter who is a constant companion when we are in the office and he can be found lying across the desk guarding my diary!

I'm sure you agree with me that your working environment is important. We may spend at least eight hours a day in our office. As a consultant we need to be focused yet have the right space for thinking creatively.

Consider carefully where you will work. Create a space that works for you whether it's the spare bedroom/dining room or a purpose-built office. The systems I share with you in the chapter on Courage will accelerate your opportunity to scale up your business. I will show you how to create a mobile consulting business that you can manage and grow wherever you are in the world.

Which brings me to my dream destination and where living and working blends into one happy combination.

The office with a sea view

As I've described previously, my office in Corfu is a desk on the balcony overlooking the sea. It's simple but so inspirational and my team all work remotely, some in the UK and other expats on mainland Greece and in Corfu. You don't need large fancy offices to be effective. The trend to work anywhere has taken off. You need a laptop, mobile phone, Wi-Fi and a printer (I still like to print).

"I wasn't made to spend my life at a desk. I was made to feel the sun on my face, walk barefoot by the ocean, and work in a way that brings freedom and joy."

I don't feel like I am working when I am sitting here – I am grateful.

Before you can get to this position though you need to create the right structure for your business. This is what we are exploring next.

A business that thrives creates wealth and time for you

Growth is one of the indicators of success for a business; the speed of the increase leads to acceleration of income and the benefits that you get. But you must create an efficient operating model too.

THREE GROWTH DRIVERS

A profit mindset, not revenue. Revenues reward your ego, but profit rewards your bank account. You need to create a profit mindset and start measuring profit growth and key indicators, such as: clear strategy, increased revenue, and reduced expenses. In the world of consulting the two keys here are charging the right fees and charging for your time accurately.

Cash that is truly flowing. A consultancy that thrives is a consultancy where money is never an issue. It is always available when it's time to invest in growth because it is generated quickly. Having an easy finance system, which we will touch upon later in the book, helps manage your cashflow.

Finally, *effectiveness*. To make it happen you should focus on areas such as leadership, smarter working, and delegation. We talk more about smarter working in Chapter 13 – Courage.

Only when you put these three factors in place can you end up wealthier thanks to a successful consulting business.

In Part 2, Chapter 10 – Clarity I talk about how to define what your niche is, how you package and price your services and how to grow your business without burnout.

INCOME STRATEGIES

These are the income strategies that you need to consider for scaling your business. Most people that join our bootcamps fall into the first category.

One to one
Often consultants get sucked into delivering services to just one person, whether it is coaching or some other service. Your reach is limited and so will be your time available and income.

One to many
The next stage from this is an approach where you are "one to many" – running events, seminars, webinars, or workshops. Your reach is much more significant, but you are spending the same amount of time to achieve this.

Many to many
A great friend and consultant reminded me recently of the "many to many" strategy where you have a sales team of affiliates or even a franchise model.

Multiple streams of income are mentioned in Part 2, Chapter 12 – Collaboration.

Moving beyond selling your time in exchange for a fee is how you accelerate the growth of your business. To do this, you will need to productise your business to scale predictably.

It has never been easier to turn your ideas into products electronically and to create online courses. These evergreen products work for you whilst you are sleeping, and your reach is worldwide. Profitability from digital products is high and this allows you to reinvest in your marketing.

It is not unusual for consultants to have a secondary stream of income from a totally unrelated business. This can be great in the early days to address financial stress. I did this - however, eventually if you want to grow your consulting business you will need to give it 100% of your time and commitment.

PART 2:
The 5C's "From Corporate to Consulting" Model

"You can't tiptoe toward transformation—dare to take the leap"

SUPERCHARGE YOUR CHANCE OF SUCCESS

I am guessing that you have a streak in you that says that you want to say you did this by yourself. All alone? I do recognise this as this was exactly how I was – asking for help felt like I hadn't done it myself and that my success was worth less.

It has taken me many years to realise both in my personal and work life that it's OK to have help and now I wouldn't be without my mentors and coaches (yes, there is more than one).

If you want to accelerate your success – and do it the easier way – why wouldn't you?

I speak to so many people that say they will "give it a go first", rather than investing in coaching or a fast-track programme. And here's the thing, yes you can give it a go, but as a consultant earning a living typically from charging by the hour or day, why waste your time trying to figure it out?

I have spent over 30 years figuring out what works and what doesn't – in a very niche market – and my way is most definitely not the only way but I know from the results my students and coachees get that it works.

WHY IS IT IMPORTANT TO GET QUICK WINS?

The last thing you need is to have a slow start and doubt yourself and ponder whether interim or going back into the corporate world would be better.

What I have learnt, more recently in the last six years as the landscape for me has changed during this time, is incorporated into my model – From Corporate to Consulting.

It is a structured way to guide you through the key areas of setting up your business, although there are other operational business matters that I cover later in the book as well.

This model has been shared with over 1000 business owners so far. The feedback that we get independently and the results our clients get prove it can work.

With all models it will evolve and adapt over time to be even better but right now this is getting results for my clients and we are all happy. You can see career transition stories and testimonials in Part 5.

THE FROM CORPORATE TO CONSULTING MODEL

Whilst we cover these 5C's in the book, we explore them in a lot more detail on our bootcamps and other coaching programmes. I have included them here (https://leap-into-consulting.mykajabi.com/products/book-downloads), with digital downloads, so that you can benefit from the content wherever you are in the world and whatever budget you have.

When you are starting out as a consultant it is easy to jump into creating an all-encompassing website and to start to market yourself as a generalist to ensure you capture as much work as possible in the early days.

What I have found working with new consultants, like you, is that there tends to be a lack of clarity in what you really want to offer clients, and who these clients are. On top of this you may not have analysed the types of problems your potential clients have and the solutions that you plan to sell them.

A lot of time and money can be wasted if the sequence is in the wrong order and this is why I developed this methodology for you to accelerate this process. It is illustrated in this diagram.

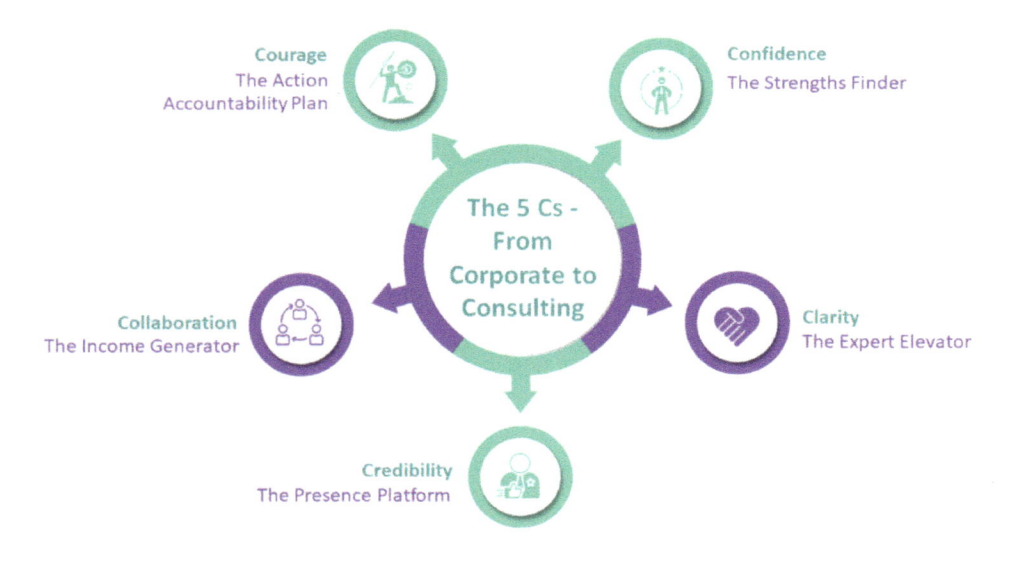

Courage — The Action Accountability Plan

Confidence — The Strengths Finder

Collaboration — The Income Generator

Clarity — The Expert Elevator

Credibility — The Presence Platform

The 5 Cs - From Corporate to Consulting

The first stage surrounds confidence and establishing what the bigger picture is for you and how your attributes, skills and experience can help you transition into consulting.

With this stage completed we then go onto Stage 2 – Clarity, where we really dig deep into the detail of what your ideal client looks like, how you will charge for your services and products and linking this into your dream reality.

With Stages 1 and 2 completed this then allows you to put this clarity into action through your marketing. Stage 3 explores the importance of your online credibility with the Presence Platform Audit, how you build your expertise and brand and how you maximise all of this to generate those clients that you want to have.

To superboost your portfolio and income this then takes you to Stage 4 – Collaboration. In this stage I outline the benefits of collaboration, how to do this and the results that you can achieve.

And finally, Stage 5 – Courage is focused on accountability: making things happen and working smarter not harder. This ranges from cloud technology to looking after yourself as a consultant and effective work habits. I share with you more information about our Accountability Community Groups and other options to keep you on track.

Chapter 9:
Confidence

The fears identified from the CIPD research mentioned earlier in the book are all underpinned by confidence.

What is confidence?

Are you living up to your full potential? The difference between a good consultant and an excellent consultant often lies in confidence.

Psychology Today defines confidence as follows[3]:

> *"Confidence is a belief in oneself, the conviction that one has the ability to meet life's challenges and to succeed – and the willingness to act accordingly. Being confident requires a realistic sense of one's capabilities and feeling secure in that knowledge.*
>
> *Projecting confidence helps people gain credibility, make a strong first impression, deal with pressure, and tackle personal and professional challenges. It's also an attractive trait, as confidence helps put others at ease."*

WHY IS CONFIDENCE IMPORTANT?

This first stage of my model is key. If you don't have confidence, everything else is going to be more difficult.

When you have confidence in your services and products and yourself this is observable to others. They will see how you are passionate about what you do; they will want to talk with you about your services and invest in you.

Confidence can come from a wide variety of sources and in the context of consulting mainly from having the expertise to deliver the project or being able to answer a client's question. As HR professionals, with several years under your belt, that is a given. You have managed complex problems, resolved many conflicts, advised, and led a team.

Transferring your confidence

So how can we ensure that you take your confidence with you as you transition into consulting? Part of the doubt that creeps in surrounds the lack of knowledge of how to run a business and as a business owner for over 30 years sometimes I forget what it was like at the beginning of my journey. I do know that today it's much easier to set up a business. The challenge is making it sustainable and viable.

Many of my "leapers" (as I like to call them) start by offering services to SMEs in their comfort zone, transferring the skills and knowledge they have acquired and bundling it up as a service for their new client – the MD of a small business.

Sick to my stomach

I remember my first few months of consulting, and in particular one occasion when I was due to deliver a workshop for senior managers. It was my first workshop solo and on a topic that wasn't an area I was an expert in. It was residential which meant I had plenty of time to listen to my inner critic and get myself into a complete stew.

I had the classic over preparation mode kicking in – writing down exactly what to ask, when to go to the flipchart, what to write (I had already pre-prepared the flipcharts), and how to respond to a variety of questions.

Looking back, it was paralysing. I worried about whether they would like me, whether I looked ok. It went on and on and on.

Today the thought of preparing to that level sends a shiver down my spine!

> *"A jug fills drop by drop."*
> The Buddha

Celebrate your successes

Building confidence gradually is a habit. Step by step you will go beyond your previous limits – you may not even notice it happening. Take action and celebrate your successes along the way.

In our community group I see posts from consultants getting frustrated with the lack of progress, so on a regular basis I ask them to post about their achievements. The list is usually comprehensive. Having a different perspective is useful to put it into context.

Identifying your strengths is part of the process of building your confidence and staying in your comfort zone (to start with).

What happens if you don't have confidence?

- You may not even get off the starting blocks – you may decide that the risk is too great and that you are better off staying where you are.
- You may take the first step and then get knocked back.
- It may slow you down from doing podcasts, webinars, and networking.
- You will undervalue your skills, capability, and the fees that you are charging.

Confidence is the foundation of making the leap. You may find the thought of running a business daunting. So, let me address these issues now, so that you can see how you can create confidence around each area. Are these some of your concerns?

Being an accountant

I speak to so many successful HR professionals that suddenly doubt themselves when they consider self-employment. I do understand this – at the end of the day having a successful business is entirely down to your capability as an expert and business owner. Unless, like me, you studied business studies at university you may not have been involved in all aspects of running a business, the real nuts and bolts. I can reassure you that from studying to setting up a business the world has moved on. I understand the principles of accounting and we studied balance sheets (assets and liabilities), and profit and loss (P&L) sheets at university.

Do you need that now? No!

If you use a cloud software package, then it is all done for you. I use Xero, but there are lots of others on the market. No double entry bookkeeping to worry about. You press a button and get an instant P&L and balance sheet; you can set up budgets, cash flow forecasts, compare like-for-like periods... it is so simple. It is aimed at the solopreneur and growing businesses and along with a down-to-earth accountant this is all you need.

Being a salesperson

Shock horror at the thought of having to promote yourself to get work.

> *"But I hate sales."*

> *"I am no good at sales."*

> *"I just want to concentrate on being an HR expert."*

I have heard them all – let's change this mindset. As a senior HR professional, you are always selling your solutions and new initiatives and persuading senior managers about making changes or tackling difficult problems. You already have a bucket load of selling skills – and it's no different when you go into consulting. You are listening to your potential clients' problems; you are suggesting solutions to meet their needs and you are focusing on the outcomes that they may achieve (if they follow your advice). Selling in the world of consulting is all about authenticity and consultative selling. You are selling yourself and your business. You are talking about your client successes; you are passionate about what you do, and you have a compelling offer for your client.

They will want to buy from you if you get this right.

The internet has made finding clients easier than ever. LinkedIn is one of my new-found areas of expertise and this is a platform bursting with opportunities. There's no selling – it's relationship building and raising your profile as an expert and authority in your area. We'll cover this in the next chapter, on Clarity.

I also run a webinar on "How to Superboost Your Consulting Profile". Details can be found here – www.leapintoconsulting.com/events.

Being a marketeer

"I don't know much about social media or how to market myself."

You know a lot more than you think. How many times have you been on LinkedIn, Facebook, websites, received a marketing email or purchased through an ad? You are surrounded by the techniques of social media marketing. Some of them resonate with you and others will switch you right off. This will help you consider how you want to approach your marketing to your ideal clients.

To get started as an HR consultant there are some foundations to what you need to do – and you can easily learn these skills. You can also easily outsource some of these aspects of your business to experts. There are plenty of options at a reasonable rate.

I am always amazed at the websites and logos that my clients design, given this isn't their prime skills set. Once you have the clarity around your name and focus of the business there are so many free resources on the internet and ways of finding new ideas about what you like and don't like.

You do not need to be an expert to get going with your marketing. We cover this more in the latter chapters.

Being an IT expert

"I am used to having an IT department to help me when it all goes wrong – I am not that tech savvy."

Let's face it, how quickly did you ever get your tech resolved?

The main elements you need to get up and running as a consultant are:

Your laptop/desktop – Make sure that you use cloud technology for everything that you do. This way you don't have issues of version control of documents or not being able to access information that you need.

I highly recommend **Office 365** as this keeps everything cloud based and always up to date. There are so many useful features on this, and it also allows you to grow a team easily. Office 365 comes with OneDrive, which backs up all your content to the cloud. There are also other cloud-based storage options that are easy to use. If you have a system or something of significant value intellectually, I will always recommend a back-up to a removable drive.

Video conferencing – Get familiar with one platform and use it full capacity. Given the expansion of video conferencing make it key to your business. It's very effective for your business and increase the scope of who you can work with.

File sharing – You will need to share files with clients and associates and the easiest way to do this is through platforms like WeTransfer. It's a free option and allows large files to be shared easily. You can also track the delivery and download status.

That's it!

Master these and you are up and running. You probably use all of these programmes and software already. Your IT support now switches to product support for each of the options you have chosen. The support you get online and via helpdesks is amazing and they are fully aware that most users are not technical experts.

They are also available online 24/7.

CONFIDENCE AROUND YOUR EXPERTISE

Earlier in the book you considered what your strengths were and what products you could create from this. This is your starting point and is often a key moment when people explore how they are going to shape their business services. You can start by offering services that play to your strengths (so you are confident) and build in new offerings over time. More on this in the next chapter on Clarity.

Operational HR

When I started as a consultant most of the work I had been involved in was operational: hundreds of employee relations issues and the opportunity to redesign policies and procedures. I worked with several area and regional managers as well as the head office functions including the HR team. This helped me build relationships with key stakeholders (no different to an MD of an SME).

The work was very transactional, but it solved some key problems that needed support for the business to thrive. There were performance issues, recruitment challenges, issues of misconduct and the list goes on.

Many of these HR matters still exist today and have become even more complex with legislation accelerating at a pace that many HR professionals find challenging, let alone business owners.

So, when you consider moving into consulting it's important to remember that you have a wealth of knowledge that you can exchange for a fee!

Your niche

After starting in operational HR services I then specialised in a number of different areas based on the work I was asked to do and the areas that interested me. You must remember I have had many years to change direction!

I have specialised in:

- Employee engagement programmes
- 360-degree feedback programmes
- Culture change
- Team building – outdoor and indoors
- HR systems implementation
- Assessment and development centres
- Competency frameworks
- Psychometric testing

None of these areas were that familiar to me when I was employed. So, go with what is right for you now and your marketplace. If your clients do not have a need for your services, because it doesn't solve a problem for them, they are unlikely to buy.

The marketplace is forever changing and you will need to be adaptable with your services to ensure you stay relevant and in demand.

Free work

Another way of building your confidence at the beginning of your journey is to provide free work and advice for friends and family, just to get feedback. It's not a strategy that will help you grow your business if you never transition into fee earning activities! The benefit of this though is you will soon realise how much people appreciate your help and support. And then you start charging.

Other topics linked to confidence

Apart from the concerns that I have just touched on there are a couple of other aspects I want to share with you.

Comfort zone

The first is about comfort zones, illustrated in the diagram below. If you are lacking confidence in any way you are likely to stay within the first circle – the comfort zone. You may even be in the fear zone right now.

Women tend to underestimate their abilities and assume the challenges are bigger than they are. It's often the first few steps that are the most difficult to take.

If you want more from life you have to step outside your comfort zone. You may have seen the image circulating on social media that suggests that outside the comfort zone is where life begins.

Can you relate to where you are on the model below?

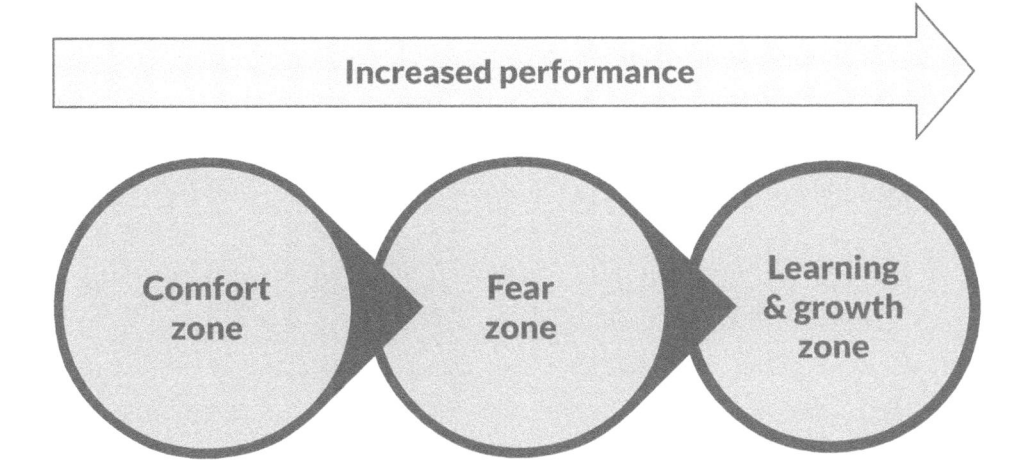

Increased performance

Comfort zone → Fear zone → Learning & growth zone

As you progress through your career as a consultant you are likely to move through these zones to the growth zone. How quickly you go through these zones will depend on how you challenge yourself and what support you have to guide you through these stages.

Start from your comfort zone and push the boundaries as quickly as you can. Having a coach and a buddy can accelerate your personal and business growth too.

A comfort zone is defined as a state where things feel familiar and you are at ease, being in control. This is where low levels of anxiety and stress are likely to occur. However, you will also know that the research has indicated that this is a zone where a steady level of performance takes place.

I am guessing that you are wanting more than this. In this case we need to step outside the comfort zone, a state where the added stress and anxiety leads to enhanced performance. There does become a point though where the additional stress becomes too much, and the performance deteriorates leading to the danger zone and burnout or other issues.

By following the structure of the "From Corporate to Consulting" Model you will build new skills and knowledge as well as building your confidence.

Let's look at a second topic that is also closely related to confidence.

Imposter syndrome

I have already mentioned this a few times including in my own story.

I am sure you will have heard this talked about in the media – it seems to be the in-thing for actors and celebrities to open up about. Most recently the acclaimed actress Jodie Comer said that she thought she had imposter syndrome because of her Liverpool accent and background. She even considered other career options because of her perception about how others would view her.

What is imposter syndrome?
Firstly, it's a complex topic and not an area I am an expert in, however these are some of the aspects that might fall under the banner:

The inner critic
Do you ever catch yourself hearing your inner voice saying these things?

"I'm not good enough."

"I might mess up."

"They are better than me."

"I must be perfect."

"I don't fit in here."

This inner voice can lead you into procrastinating or over preparing, with a high level of anxiety. And as a consultant delivering a project for your client this may impact on your efficiency. If you do five drafts to get it perfect, how long is this taking? It's unlikely you can charge your client for this extra time, so you'll find yourself in a situation where you are not billing enough hours.

"The longer you wait, the steeper it feels —take the first step now."

Imposter Syndrome

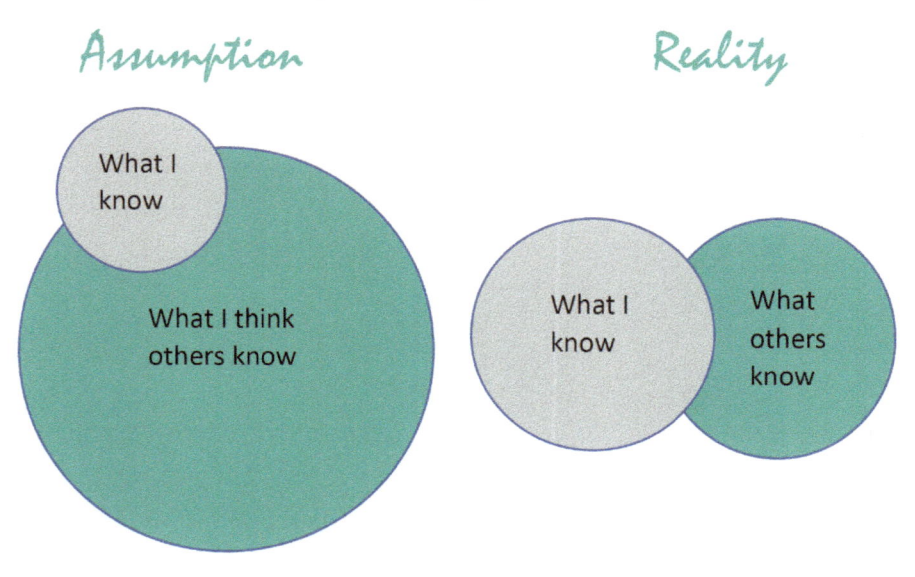

Assumption

- What I know
- What I think others know

Reality

- What I know
- What others know

Often, as illustrated in the diagram above, how we see the world and the reality can be very different. For many that identify with imposter syndrome they assume that what they know is much less than what they think their peer group know, when in reality it is likely to be very similar.

As a consultant with imposter syndrome are you likely to accept the feedback from your client when they say how delighted they are with your work – or are you going to brush it off?

I am not one for labels, so being labelled as someone suffering from imposter syndrome doesn't work for me. What we can take from this, though, is to unpick what is happening when you are getting these feelings:

What are you learning from the feelings you are getting?

Is it worth acknowledging it and then moving on?

Or is it a "that belongs in the bin" – as it's just not true?

Perspective

I spoke with a "soon to be" consultant recently and she was expressing her concern about professional indemnity insurance as she was worried about what would happen if her advice was wrong. I explored this a little further with her to discover that in her 10 years of advising her current employer she had never made an error of judgement. The chances of this changing when she is self-employed are low, and once this level of awareness took place, I could tell that the new perspective on the matter had changed her concerns about the risks.

One of the exercises I recommend as part of your journey into consulting is completing your Wheel of Life. This provides some context to what is happening holistically for you and to see how consulting might redress the balance, where needed.

As a mother and business owner, as well as a partner, there are often lots of conflicting pulls on my time. I have also found that on occasions through my consulting journey, when I stop and reflect because I feel out of balance, I return to this exercise and it soon becomes apparent what I need to do to redress this.

If you are passionate about your business, it is very easy to get overly focused on it to the detriment of other aspects of your life. If you speak to many successful entrepreneurs, they find that they have regrets about not spending enough time with their family or partner, often feeling they have missed out on their children's lives.

Many of us went into consulting to get more time with our children but I also recognise that this means being present, not just physically!

This next exercise has created a lot of "aha" moments on our courses and I hope it does the same for you too.

THE WHEEL OF LIFE

Let's take a holistic look at what is happening right now for you.

You may have used the Wheel of Life exercise (as in the completed example shown here) before in your career. Our students find it a useful activity on our programmes where we ask them to reflect on the balance of what is happening in their life. We often talk about keeping work and home life separate but as a consultant the two are one.

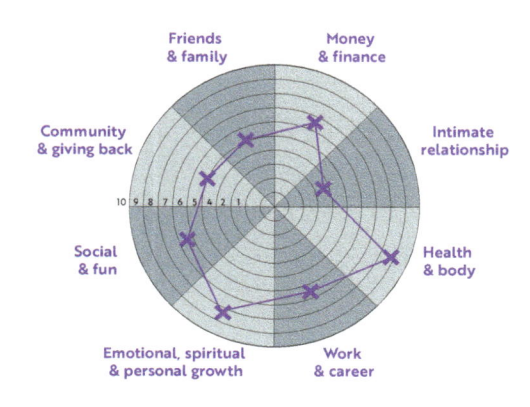

Below is a template for you to look at the key aspects of your life and rate them on a scale of 1 to 10.

- 1 being: I don't have this happening in my life currently or if I have it's not great.
- 10 being: I've got this in abundance and maybe too much of it at the expense of something else.

Step 1. Mark yourself against each of the criteria on a scale of 1 to 10.

Step 2. Reflect on each of these areas and consider how this is impacting your current life and wellbeing.

Step 3. Create an action plan using the table provided to address the imbalance of your wheel; after all, if this was a wheel and you had the diagram above, it would be a wonky wheel and it would be unbalanced and out of kilter.

This activity of reflection, while simple, can bring up some profound insights. I recommend that you do this whenever you're feeling a little bit out of balance or stuck and not sure what is going on.

You can of course create your own wheel with your own factors on it and if you do this that's great, however just remember it needs to be a balanced wheel with all aspects of your life in there.

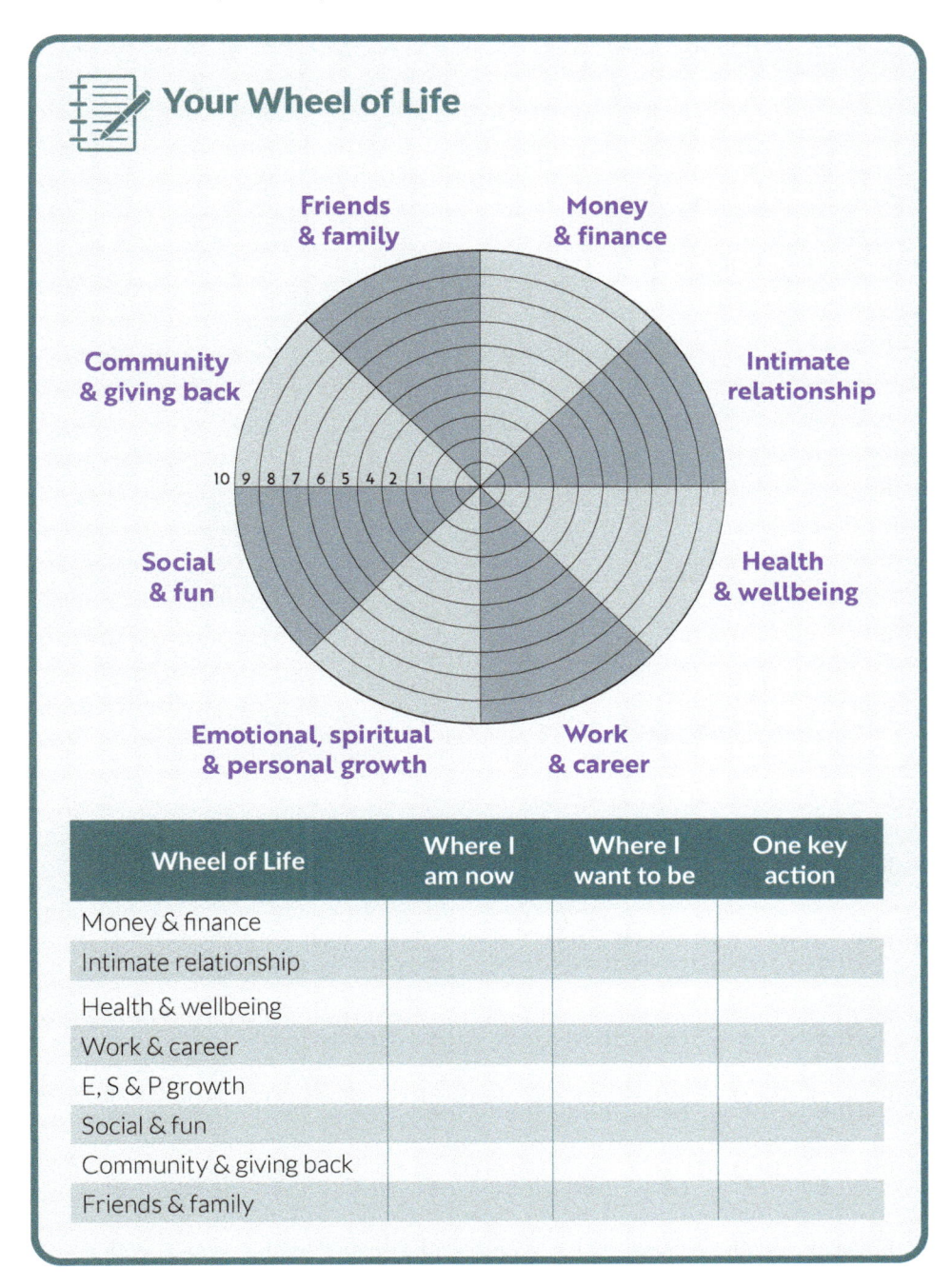

Your Wheel of Life

Segments (clockwise from top-left): Friends & family, Money & finance, Intimate relationship, Health & wellbeing, Work & career, Emotional, spiritual & personal growth, Social & fun, Community & giving back.

Scale: 10 9 8 7 6 5 4 3 2 1

Wheel of Life	Where I am now	Where I want to be	One key action
Money & finance			
Intimate relationship			
Health & wellbeing			
Work & career			
E, S & P growth			
Social & fun			
Community & giving back			
Friends & family			

When reflecting on the above exercise how is it making you feel?

_____
_____
_____
_____
_____
_____
_____
_____
_____

Action points

- [x] _____
- [x] _____
- [x] _____
- [x] _____
- [x] _____

Chapter 10:
Clarity

In this chapter you will be guided through a series of self-reflection activities to enable you to gain clarity for yourself. This starts with your why, your mission and your goals – looking at the bigger picture.

The first part of this is reflecting on what is important to you – holistically.

The dream reality

This section is about dreaming big! What are your long-term goals? Do you want to live somewhere else in the world or travel, or work three days a week doing high value work? Write a book? (We all have a book inside us.)

Maybe you have achieved many of these dreams, in which case let's go to the next level.

And the word that can't be mentioned ... MONEY! How much do you want to earn? Be bold.

Finally, how much energy have you got to do all of this? Because it takes energy to make a business grow – but it's about working SMARTer, not harder.

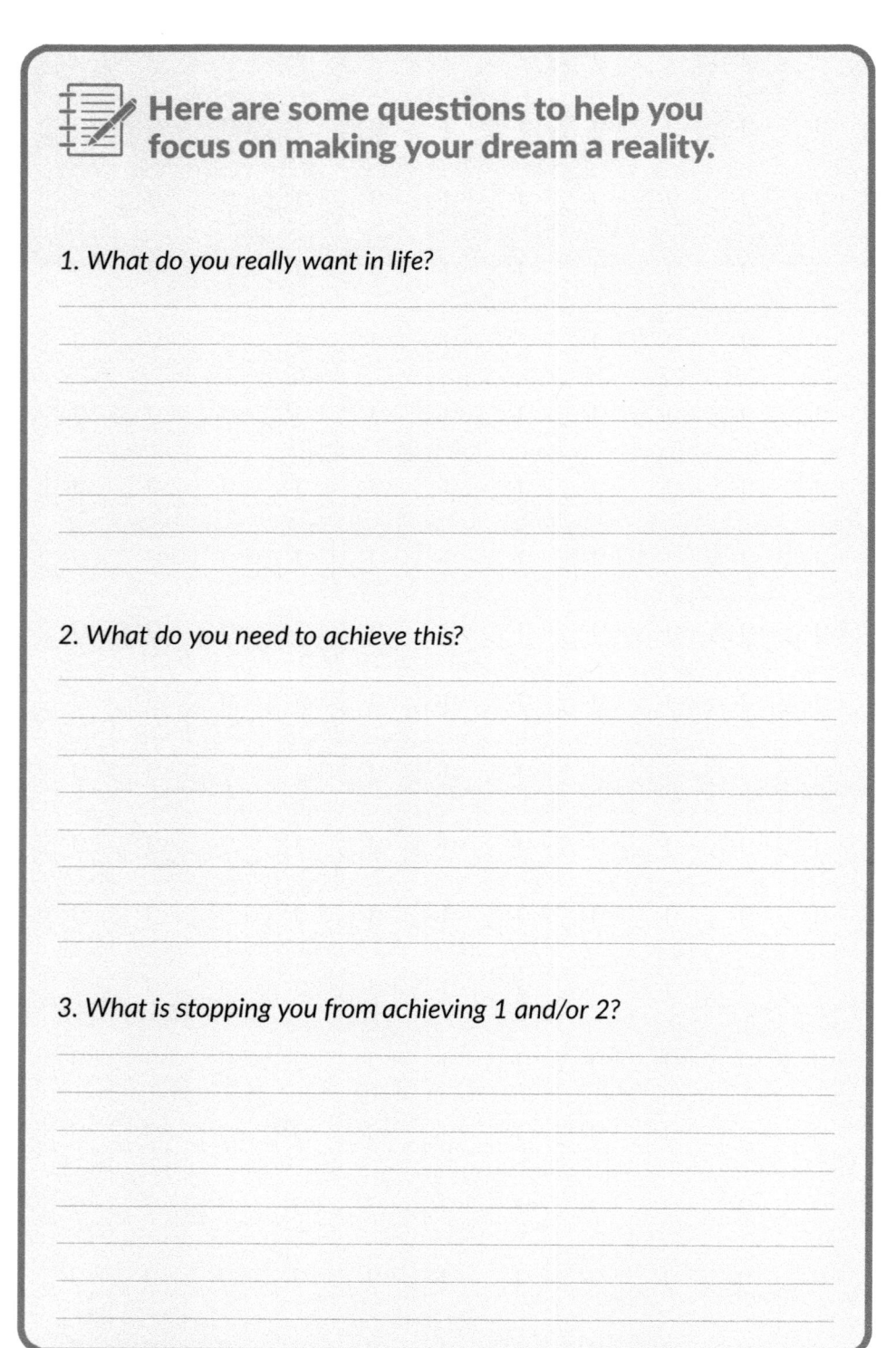

Here are some questions to help you focus on making your dream a reality.

1. What do you really want in life?

2. What do you need to achieve this?

3. What is stopping you from achieving 1 and/or 2?

Action points

- [ ] _____
- [ ] _____
- [ ] _____
- [ ] _____
- [ ] _____

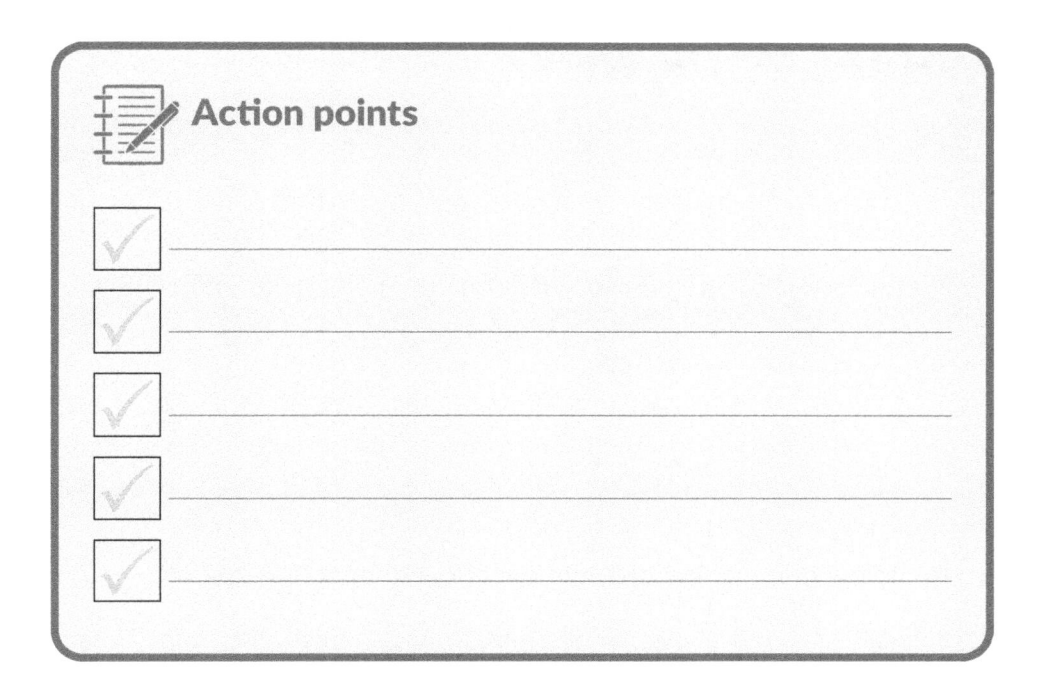

With your clarity and the actions that you are planning to take this will lead you to achieve your results. Even if you take the first steps this will move you forward.

Clarity + Inspired Action = Results

WHAT'S YOUR WHY?

Your consulting business is you! People will work with you because they want to, not because of your education or your qualifications.

What have you achieved to date that you can share with your clients?
- What are your passions?
- What do you love doing?
- Where do you feel you can really add value to potential clients?
- Where have you had feedback from your line managers or from people you've worked with within the organisations about what you're really known for?
- When people talk about you what do they remember you for?

Just think about what makes you want to jump out of bed in the morning, because the more you focus your attention on your passions the more energy you'll have, and this will be portrayed in the work that you do with your clients.

The last thing clients want is to work with miserable consultants, trust me. They are sadly sometimes surrounded by enough people that are miserable; they don't need more.

In my experience clients enjoy my upbeat positive nature and a "can do" attitude. Nothing is too much trouble. How do I do this? It's because I love what I do and am passionate about helping others.

If you don't love what you do how will you inspire others to be engaged? And to be brutally frank, if you are not passionate about your work then maybe you need to rethink what you will consult about.

If you hate the transactional approach to HR, then don't set up your business around this type of work. However, you may have to start with some of this until you build your ideal client base and then you can focus more on your other areas of interest.

Consulting is forever evolving, and you will find that your services, interests, and the market will change. You will need to remain flexible and be aware of these shifting trends. With the internet this is easy to do, and the more clients you have in your niche the more you will get to understand what the challenges are for them.

And why you?

When you meet a potential client, either face to face or on social media, they will be asking themselves the question "What can you do to help me?" and "How are you going to solve my problem?" This is why clarity is so important – you need to grab people's attention and also know when to say that they are not the right client for you. This is where one liners can be so useful.

An example of my one liner is: "I work with ambitious professionals wanting to move from senior HR roles to being successful self-employed HR consultants."

It is worth having a one liner – this can be used for marketing strap lines or simply replying when someone asks you what you do. You can build upon this and talk about your story. We all have a story that will resonate for others.

Your story – exercise and questions
As a consultant your success is much more than your products and services, it's also about sharing yours or your clients' story, a true story, to build rapport with your new potential clients and for them to get to know you. If they are interested in you, they are likely to be interested in your services too.

When you use a story to describe what life was like before your clients found the solution and how it is now for them you will be describing the pain points and desires of your clients.

If you speak to your potential clients now, they are likely to say that they are OK and there is no need to change anything. Through hearing your story and the work that you do for others they might realise that they too have a problem that you can solve for them.

There is a lot of hype about using stories in marketing and my top tip would be to be authentic. You are not stupid, nor are your clients, and they will be able to spot from a mile off if it's a made-up story and then your credibility will be undermined.

If you share stories well, your clients will probably be eager to hear how clients went from before to after. They are looking for the "golden nugget" they can use to change their life and business. You're going to offer them access to the "golden nugget".

My why and story
My purpose is to enable other people to create the freedom and flexibility they want through successfully setting up their own consultancy.

You will have already read a lot about my story earlier in the book. Now let's look at your story.

Your story

We all have a story that has shaped where we are now – it often underpins why we do what we do. The following questions should help you pin down what yours is, and how this influences your potential as an HR consultant.

What is your story?

How does this shape the products and services that you want to offer?

How does your story help your potential clients?

Your talents and passions

From reflecting on your personal story it's now time to review your business career and look at the transferable skills and knowledge you have for consulting.

In the last three years of your role, or even in the last 12 months, what projects or programmes have you delivered successfully?

These are large projects or programmes – not day-to-day operational matters.

Project & problems you have solved	Solutions you delivered	Outcomes & ROI
e.g. Underperformance across the business	Revised performance management programme	Increase from 40%–80% completed reviews Employee engagement survey – improved results

Project & problems you have solved	Solutions you delivered	Outcomes & ROI

It's useful to look at the whole scope of the programme that you've delivered. What was the purpose? What was the desired outcome for this project? How did you go about delivering the project? How did you manage the project? How did you communicate with the project? How did you evaluate the success of that project? What was the return on investment? Did you even look at the return on investment? If you didn't then it's important that you start looking at how to evaluate and quantify your successes in what you do.

Metrics and technology are two key elements that MDs will look to you to prove that what you do works.

Think about the other outcomes that you've achieved to date as well. What awards have you put yourself forwards for or have you been nominated for?

What other interesting activities do you do outside of work that would have an impact in terms of how you add value to your clients?

Many of my colleagues who do well as consultants also have a very good balanced life outside of work. Maybe you're a trustee on a board of directors, or maybe there are other things that you have done in a volunteering capacity.

Get passionate about wanting to work with lots of different clients. Start looking at business news if you're not already, pick beneath what's going on with particular companies, look at what the growth markets are, and look at where your niche might be. This is the time for you to decide where best you're suited. I know for example from my own experience that whilst I've loved some of the programmes that I delivered in the public sector, that isn't where my heart lies; my heart lies in growing SMEs that are passionate about growing their businesses and are small enough that I can make a big impact in their organisation. That's my passion, so what's your passion? Play to your strengths.

It's interesting that you might find that what you thought was your ideal client and type of services aren't what excite you. As well as defining your ideal client it's about defining your niche.

You need to stand out from the crowd because there are thousands of consultants out there. You need to define the "one thing" that makes you unique.

Your expert positioning will mean you are in front of the right clients. You will be creating content that people will want to read, and they will want to seek advice from you. They will open your emails because they are interesting and relevant.

In the last three years I have invested thousands of pounds in self-development and training to learn more about marketing. I have taken the learnings from these events and added this to my own experience within the consulting world.

Here's my take on clarity and how it relates to setting up an HR consultancy business.

Have a "niche"

Become an expert in one area and know the problem that you are solving. This doesn't mean to say you only have this as your service, but this is what you will be known for. Being an HR generalist may be what you are but this needs to be packaged in a way that your ideal client will be attracted to your services. As you grow and evolve so will your business and as you saw in the previous chapter, I have changed my niche on a number of occasions.

I started as an outsourced HR service for local SMEs and then evolved into competency frameworks, then developed a 360-degree feedback system, then employee engagement and now I focus on coaching others to set up their business. It's important to note that my transition and change was over a 30-year period, so it's important not to chop and change every two minutes, causing confusion for your existing clients.

When you are clear on your niche, you can be clear on your marketing.

What your ideal client looks like

Be specific about who your ideal client is. It doesn't matter if this is a business to business relationship or consumer relationship; this still needs detailed analysis. And when you think you have enough detail you probably don't. It's a forever evolving piece of research. Talking and getting to know your clients will elicit this for you. You don't have to ask them even; they will share information with you quite freely.

When I changed my focus from consulting to coaching consultants my ideal client changed totally. So, from MDs of SMEs in Hampshire, Dorset and central London I now work with HR professionals looking to move into consulting. As you will see when you do this exercise for yourself you can drill down into a lot more detail. When you start defining your ideal client you then need to see whether this hypothesis is true and is right for you and your services. This only comes with time and feedback and market research.

What happens if you don't have clarity?

If you don't have clarity there are a number of potential consequences which I have highlighted below.

The art of being distracted
In the start-up phase of your business you are likely to be keen to say yes to every opportunity: networking, meetings, client work etc. The danger with this is that it can make you busy, but not productive, and it's easy to get distracted when you don't have clarity and focus.

Getting the wrong clients
Don't get me wrong, saying no to a paying client can be difficult but if you have the wrong clients it will create more heartache down the line. If your diary is full of lower fee-paying clients that aren't your niche, then the chances are that you then won't have space left for those you would like to work with and who would pay you what you are worth.

How do you make the decision as to whether they are the right client?
Are they in your niche, do they fit your ideal client profile, and most importantly do they have a set of values that are in line with yours?

If the client makes you question whether they are going to be a good client, they probably won't be. Use your intuition; it's usually right and over time you will be able to spot the red flags of working with clients that fall into this category.

A business colleague and I recently reflected on a client we had both worked with. We loved working with this client but faced the same challenges with the MD. All the attributes that lead to being an entrepreneur are often the polar opposite to what you need to be compliant with Employment Law, or any other law.

Also ask yourself the question about whether you would want to build a long-term relationship with them. Most of my clients have worked with me for over 10 years. If I take a client on, I want to add value by really understanding them and their business. This takes time and it's like the issue of staff turnover; you really don't want to be recruiting new clients all the time. Nurture the ones you have. It's rewarding and more profitable.

"What do you do?"

Without clarity this can become a rambling moment at a networking event. For years people have been talking about your elevator pitch – a short snappy introduction. I once did this exercise with a business owner that lived in the Middle East and given there were 173 floors in the tallest building there, his 30 second elevator pitch went on for nearly 5 minutes!

If you have experienced BNI (a networking group in the UK that meets at the crack of dawn weekly), then you will have heard many one-minute summaries.

Of course, you may have more than one ideal client, like I do, so it depends who you are talking to as to which hat you wear.

Clarity is important to be able to articulate what you do.

> *Knowing what you do is important for you and your clients.*

The Expert Elevator we talk about in our bootcamps is designed to elevate you to the role of being an expert because you must stand out in the consulting marketplace.

The Expert Elevator is a simple, straightforward exercise that shows you the one thing that you should be shouting about from the rooftops. You need to stand out from the crowd, because different is always perceived as better.

It is vital that you have identified it correctly – that one thing. It cuts through everything and underneath all of that is the shiny diamond that is yours to present to the world.

I found it difficult to scale my business after a certain point, given that I was working on the model of charging for consulting time. And then I stumbled upon "the thing" for me. Overnight I went from having a business that was restricted by a time for money model to creating an online product that had worldwide reach and with many concurrent users.

It wasn't an overnight success for me, and you too could create a secret sauce that generates passive income. In Chapter 12 – Collaboration I will share with you how you can create products and passive income.

If only I had had help to see this earlier, it would have made my life so much easier.

I would have attracted more work faster and easier. I wouldn't have had to struggle so much with working long hours.

And when you have that secret sauce:

- Your status is instantly elevated as you stand apart because of that one thing.
- It makes you money whilst you sleep, because your product is out there.
- It attracts business to you – without you doing so much work.

It can become a product that **monetises for you** – that means you're making money without running around. **How would that feel?**

New clients are coming to you, and you don't have to work so hard to bring business in?

Web-based 360-degree feedback

My 360 product is licensed to now sell in 56 countries. It started off as a solution to one client's problem.

When this client asked us to do a 360-degree feedback programme in the late 1990s it was a relatively new concept in the UK. A well-known bank approached us to run their 100 leaders through the process, using their competencies. Amazing news? You would have thought so, wouldn't you?

Then the detail emerged. We couldn't use electronic means; it needed to be paper based for security reasons within the banking sector.

We had over 1000 pieces of paper returned to our office, all pre-coded, and then we had to extract the data manually and create the reports. It was successful for the client, but we ploughed a vast amount of resources into the project and made a loss.

What did we learn from this? We realised that there was probably a demand for this with other clients, so we developed an Excel-based questionnaire and then a few years later developed a fully web-based system (it would now be classified as an SaaS). We had a team of developers in India and invested much of our profits back into the system to create a product.

This process was complex, at times extremely frustrating, and created equal amounts of excitement as well as fear in our business.

When you discover that secret sauce it's easy – easiest thing in the world – but you could overlook and undervalue it. It must be easy for everyone to discover. The truth is this is the thing that you charge the most for. This is your diamond. It's so critical.

Let's get some answers for you quickly rather than waiting, like I did for many years. I will return to this later in the book.

Same old, same old

There may be the temptation to do the same type of work, in the same type of business or sector because as I have mentioned before it is in your comfort zone.

This can feel like a shift from working for one employer to working with many, but you may then start to feel unfulfilled as this was the type of work you wanted to get away from.

If you are not happy as a consultant, it normally falls into three areas:

1. You are working with clients that you don't enjoy working with, whether they have different values, or a personality that you just find awkward.

2. The work you are doing isn't fulfilling or uplifting or it may be outside of your comfort zone e.g. redundancies and disciplinaries.

3. The way that you are working is making you unhappy e.g. extensive travel, long hours, staying away from home, being interrupted in the evening and weekends.

Reviewing these factors on a regular basis will steer you towards the kinds of projects that you enjoy and the type of clients that you want to work with. It's OK to say no to clients and to walk away (in a professional manner), if it's not working out.

Looking explicitly at these factors and their contribution to your satisfaction with the consulting life is the first step in going after the kinds of projects and clients that you will enjoy. It's ok to do this as part of your strategy to transition if you have a plan to expand out of your comfort zone to do the work you are passionate about in the future.

If you don't it's a lot of effort to run a business when you are not excited by what you are doing nor do you feel rewarded fully.

Your clients will notice this as well. Sometimes it's important to re-evaluate your offering before it gets to this point. As noted earlier, I have pivoted my services several times through the years.

Most recently I have moved away from spending as much time with consulting clients to coaching and mentoring HR professionals. It's a big shift for me but my energy and motivation are much more aligned. Helping other people like you set up and grow your consulting business is so rewarding. Seeing results within weeks is what drives me to be even better.

> *"The goal is not to do business with everyone who needs what you have. The goal is to do business with people who believe what you believe."*
> Simon Sinek

WHO IS YOUR IDEAL CLIENT?

Having real clarity of your ideal client is important to be able to target your marketing efforts and spend. This is essential so that you can create your social media including your website. Does it talk to your ideal client?

Who's your ideal client – and what is their problem – what is the frustration of their problem not being solved?

I love the analogy about the painkillers and the vitamins.

> We all know that if you take vitamins longer term your health will be better, but we often don't take them even though we know this is good for us.
>
> But we do take painkillers when we need to get rid of pain – we actively seek them.
>
> If your solutions are "painkillers" then people will be actively searching for you.
>
> If you have a "vitamin" business solution you will have to sell to people what you do.

The more detail the better. So, for example is your ideal client a male aged 30–48, living in Hampshire, with the job title Managing Director, number of employees 50–200, a person that is open minded and has an interest in personal development, and plays golf in his spare time?

This level of detail is important: if you don't know what your ideal clients' interests are and where they hang out in the business community, then every time you talk to a potential ideal client ask questions about them, and you will soon build up your own market research.

If you already have clients, then explore more with them about their interests. What books do they read, where do they like to visit, what hobbies do they have? The more detail the better.

It is also important to understand what your ideal client wants.

International bestseller and coach Fiona Harrold mentioned in her programme "The Expert Formula" 9 of the most common drivers of potential clients:

1. They want to be healthy.
2. They want to be more popular and impress people.
3. They want to be more attractive.
4. They want meaningful relationships.
5. They want to be secure and set up for life.
6. They want things to be easy.
7. They want more free time.
8. They want to feel like they're accomplishing things.
9. They want more income.

She highlights that you need to dig deeper into the desires of your prospect to craft a message that resonates with their subconscious and conscious desires. You will not hit all of them with your product, but the aim is to meet three or four.

You can also download our IDEAL client worksheet to complete at this link: https://leap-into-consulting.mykajabi.com/products/book-downloads.

Many consultants worry about being creative with social media. There are plenty of sites that you can use free of charge for templates (for example canva.com), to ensure you are creative – but **clarity** is more important at this stage.

Be clear and complete the worksheet before you start spending time or money on marketing, including your LinkedIn profile or website.

You may have more than one ideal client, in which case repeat the exercise for each one.

If you are a visual person and creative, then think of your ideal client and create a vision board so that you have it to hand when looking at content writing.

YOUR CLIENT'S PAIN POINTS

As I have highlighted already unless your client has a pain point or real desire, they are unlikely to want to buy anything. Here are a few of the questions to ask yourself about your ideal client.

- What personal pain will you solve?
- What causes your client the most headaches?
- Your client will only buy if you are solving a pain for them. What's the cost of this pain and what solutions can you offer your client?
- What are you especially good at, and passionate about?
- What business pains can you solve for your clients?
- Which causes the greatest harm, risk, or danger to your clients?
- How much is this pain costing your client per month?
- What is the perfect solution to this pain your prospect is experiencing?
- What will you offer your client to solve this for your client?
- How much will it cost?

Some examples of client pains:

- The pain of not having an efficient system for HR admin and not being able to find the information they need easily
- The pain of having untrained managers leading your teams creating employee relations problems and grievances
- The pain of not being able to attract the right candidates to the company
- The pain of too many staff leaving in the first six months of joining the business.

It costs the client time and money to solve these problems – the hard way. You have the easy way because you have the experience to solve for them. It's probably your bread and butter knowledge.

So, what can you bring to the party?

Clarity of offering

Your niche and buyer's psychology

To succeed, you must be solving a problem that is an urgent and pressing problem for your ideal client **right now**.

This is not any problem; this is the problem that keeps them awake at night – *it is your client's "HELL"*.

There are so many problems that exist now in business – brainstorm these URGENT people problems that need solving.

List the people problems – your ideal client's "HELL".

Now – urgent	Some other key changes e.g. IR35

The clue to knowing what that hell is lies in your ideal client, in the head and heart of the person you want to serve.

Knowing your niche is one thing, the group of people you want to serve, but understanding the psychology and deep needs of this person is what will allow you to speak their language.

Step inside the shoes of your ideal client (using your completed client worksheet), and see and feel the world through their eyes.

Turn the answers into headline questions using simple language that people use when they think and speak to themselves.

Example

Sally, 36, is an HR manager.

She is the ideal client for Sarah, a coach who works with consultants and experts to help them transition from corporate life to consulting.

Getting inside Sally's head, Sarah can see the following:

> *What is your biggest worry right now?*
> I do not get the flexibility I need.
>
> *What is your biggest frustration right now?*
> Juggling work and childcare.
>
> *What is your biggest fear right now?*
> I will never be able to be there for my children.

Headline questions

> *Do you worry that you do not have the flexibility that you want?*
> *Are you juggling work and childcare?*
> *Are you scared that you will not be there for your children?*

This is the conversation Sally is having in her head right now. By reflecting this back to her, in the simple language she uses in her head and to speak, Sarah is showing that she understands her problem precisely.

This is when people say,

> *"I feel like you're in my head."*
> *"You're a mind reader."*
> *"You've been reading my thoughts."*

Get clear on your ideal client

Ask them these questions. Turn their answers into headline questions that you can use on your website, in your webinars, workshops, and writing. Wow them with your uncanny insight and understanding!

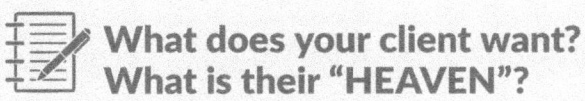

What does your client want?
What is their "HEAVEN"?

What do they dream of, desire, need, to be successful?

So how are you going to get your client from a place of despair to their desired place?

(These are your solutions and products – your offers)

Ideas for starter offer

_____
_____
_____
_____
_____

Ideas for mid-level offer

_____
_____
_____
_____
_____

Ideas for high value offer

_____
_____
_____
_____
_____

What are the steps for them?

Make it clear and easy for them to buy.

1. _____

2. _____

3. _____

4. _____

5. _____

Next …

What transformations are your product or services going to give to your ideal client if they successfully put your solution into action?

1. _____

2. _____

3. _____

4. _____

5. _____

As a transformational leader you are responsible for creating transformation change with your ideal clients.

Ultimately this is in line with your WHY, your purpose.

Consequences when your marketing is unfocused and doesn't work

- You go unseen and unheard – clients can't find you and your true value is not potentialised.

- You feel dissatisfied and unfulfilled when you are not having a purposeful impact on clients – you question whether consulting is for you.

- You play small – you are not able to change lives and create a better world. After all, isn't that what we are ultimately doing?

BRINGING IT ALL TOGETHER

It's important to combine your talents and passions with your ideal client's pain points to create your consulting sweet spot. It's also not possible to stay in the sweet spot all the time and we must often compromise with the clients we work with and the type of work that we do.

Whilst your ideal client may remain consistent, over time their pain points will change. It's a bit like playing that childhood game, whack-a-mole. You solve one problem and then another appears.

Many of your clients will become more aware of the value of your work as they see the benefits to their business.

Start small – changing their world in one go will be too much for some and unrealistic for you to deliver.

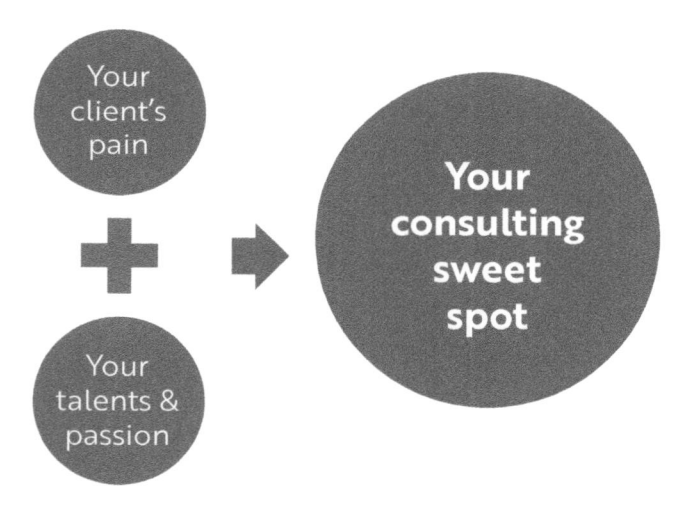

So, having gained clarity around your offerings I will now share with you how you get clarity around charging for them.

HOW DO YOU CHARGE FOR YOUR SERVICES?

A question that I get asked all the time by consultants is how much should I charge for my time?

The answer to that depends on your experience, your target market and how much you think you are worth. As a starter, if you are an independent consultant you need to work out what your hourly rate and daily rates are.

This of course is based on the model of charging for your time, which will always be capped based on the finite number of hours in a week. So, you need other income streams to complement this, as I have touched on earlier in the book.

Once you have done this, research what other similar consultants are charging. Do not undervalue yourself. You need to be confident to talk to potential clients about your fees especially when someone asks you how much you charge! You need to sell on the value you bring, not the price you charge but that's a long-term goal as most clients don't think like that.

If this worries you then practise with your family, or if they aren't the right people to do this with, practise saying it out aloud – until you convince yourself that you are worth it!

You should not be charging less than *£95 per hour (based in 2025)*.

Do you have negative beliefs about money? If you do these usually originate in childhood.

Here are some of the most common limiting beliefs about money:

- Money is the root of all evil.
- Money is not that important.
- Money is there to be spent.
- The rich get richer and the poor get poorer.
- I'm just not good with money.
- Money is a limited resource.
- You must work (too) hard to get wealthy.
- It's selfish to want a lot of money.

If you believe any of these then you must change the way you think about money. These beliefs will shape how you handle your financial life and create a reality aligned to these beliefs.

All these beliefs can be turned on their head:

- Money is an exchange for the value that you give to others.
- Money is a priority for me, to enable me to support myself and my family.
- The money I don't spend can be reinvested.
- My financial reality is entirely my responsibility.
- I am learning the skills to be better at managing finances.
- There is enough money to provide financial security for me.
- The money I have earned is because I have added value to other people.

By reframing these beliefs, you will start to create a new better reality.

Do you have any limiting beliefs about money?

Maybe you have empowering money beliefs that create an abundance of money in your life. Or maybe there is something that is still holding you back?

Complete these two sentences to find your beliefs about money:

1. I'm not financially free, because …

_____
_____
_____
_____
_____
_____

2. I'd love to have more money, but …

_____
_____
_____
_____
_____
_____

For me, the turning point about my own limiting beliefs about money was the one statement, "The money that I have earned is due to the value I have given other people".

Day rates

We have touched on this before in Chapter 3. One of the standard ways of charging is time based – by the hour, half day, or day rate.

This quick calculator (pictured below) is a rough guide as to what you may need to charge per hour to achieve your annual salary. There are of course lots of other aspects to add into this but it's a start.

For example, using the formula below if I want to earn £60k per year, my hourly rate needs to be £95 per hour, assuming I am working 5 days a week, 8 hours a day.

The reality is that you are unlikely to work all these hours as you will have to work on business activities as well. This means you either need to charge more or you must have other strategies for generating income beyond charging for your time.

Billable hours

Most consulting firms work on billable hours and this is something I also monitored more closely when I had a larger team of consultants.

Typically, if you have administration support there is an expectation that you will bill at about 80% of your time. I have worked on 60% billable and 40% working on the business, but for this to be sustainable you need to price your products and services so that you have good margins.

This is where you need to look at the following:

- Consulting based services (based on your time)
- Bundling your services as a "gift set"
- Products and online evergreen programmes
- Referral partnerships

We will revisit partnerships and evergreen programmes in Chapter 12 – Collaboration.

We will explore these in more detail in Chapter 13 – Courage.

High value, low volume or low value, high volume?

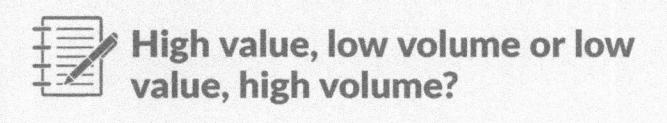

You can either spend a huge amount of time charging £195 per coaching session and need 20 clients per month to reach your income targets or charge £1950 for a high value service and need 2 clients.

What are you thinking right now?

OK, you need to believe that you are worth it, and that your services have been designed to add value to your clients.

Prada handbags

A brilliant insight I heard recently was "Don't sell a £2k product to a person that doesn't buy £2k products". If you do, they will have buyer's remorse and before you know it, they will be trying to unravel their purchase.

If it's hard work to "sell" to someone then you need to walk away from them as a client. Clients that resonate with you and your approach, when you are being authentic, are your ideal clients. Now I am realistic enough to know that when you are starting up or growing your business you will end up kissing a lot of frogs before you get your prince!

They're not my ideal client

Learn from the clients that are not your ideal clients. What do you notice about them? Why are they not the right clients for you? All clients are great learning opportunities, and the beauty of consulting is that you are not employed by your clients so it may well be a short-term relationship.

PRICING – SUMMARY PAGE

It's good to see a snapshot of your products and pricing model. What bundles have you got for your ideal client? How will you scope out your retainer agreement?

By Time:

Hourly rate (Pay as you go)	Day rate	Half-day rate
£	£	£

By Products & Packages:

	Pricing
Package / Bundle 1:	£
Package / Bundle 2:	£
Package / Bundle 3:	£

By Retainer Package:

What it includes	Pricing
	£

What is extra	Pricing
	£

What is excluded

Visit https://leap-into-consulting.mykajabi.com/products/book-downloads to download the PDF.

By now you will have explored lots of aspects of your life and potential business. You may feel you need to revisit this again later. That's OK – this is your first draft!

WHERE DO YOU FIND YOUR IDEAL CLIENTS?

Where locally (or nationally depending on your plans) can you network with your ideal clients?

I've suggested a few to start with.

	HR professionals	MDs/Owners of SMEs	Partners/ Collaboration
Face to face	Local CIPD events, even if you are not a member	Institute of Directors	CIPD exhibitions
Online	LinkedIn groups:	Chamber of Commerce	HR related products

It is easy in the early days to have a scattergun approach to networking. You do need to be laser-like with your time and attention. Check out the likely turnout at events and whether it will be full of the right people. You may be able to attend a lot of networking events as a guest free of charge for a couple of meetings to see how you get on.

Eventbrite also showcases events in your area and is a good place to look.

Networking

Networking isn't a jolly with a nice meal, it is where you are showcasing yourself with potential clients, associates, or partners. Everyone you meet knows someone that may need HR advice, eventually. I hear many people talk about "bad leads". There is no such thing as a bad lead. Please remember at networking events that they are all people with needs. They may not be your needs but treating them with respect is the right approach. There is no place for rudeness in business.

Every person you meet judges you in three seconds. How you conduct yourself, how you dress, your body language, and your handshake will all impact on this.

Be sure to have clarity around what your services are for your clients and be able to articulate them well. Practise, video yourself, get people that you respect to offer feedback. Be polished but also be you! For example, anyone who knows me well will know that you will always see me wearing a variety of shades of turquoise and blues. I am remembered for this; it's even got to the stage where people send me photos of turquoise items they have spotted whilst out and about and think I will like! It's that uniqueness that you need to find. It may sound trivial but it's busy out there; people have full minds and you need to be remembered.

Reflection

Action points

- [x]
- [x]
- [x]
- [x]
- [x]

Chapter 11: Credibility

A business owner and friend of mine recently commented, "You are all over social media – wherever I look there you are!"

I take this as compliment as you need to stand out and have a presence.

Why is credibility important?

Having a consistent and professional presence both online and face to face underpins whether people will trust you, believe you and ultimately buy from you.

It's not like the early days of my career where it was not possible to find out much about the person you might work with. Just imagine for one minute life as a consultant without the internet. It's hard to think back to those days and how it was possible to grow a business. It was possible but it wasn't easy.

Life has moved on and for you this is good news, but it also makes you much more visible. I can find out so much information about you as an individual before I have even picked up the phone. Access to public information is easy and so with this in mind it's important to review your online presence and your credibility.

The work you have done to clarify your offering will support creating a consistent approach.

However, what happens if you confuse your potential clients? They are unlikely to buy from you.

Confused people don't buy
Anything that causes people to question what you do, who you are, or your professionalism will make them back away. When clients are looking at you, you mustn't create a reason for them to hesitate. Because people are busy, they won't look further.

How many times have you gone to buy something and then hesitated? We get distracted and forget to go back and rarely do. On social media we have only seconds to grab attention.

LinkedIn is an example. When I go through profiles as part of my preparation for my LinkedIn webinars, I review the profiles of the attendees. Often consultants talk to me about how they are needing to grow their business and they are finding it difficult. I can see why.

Here are some of the common confusions I have come across:

- HR consultant / Seeking new opportunities in their headline – *So what is your focus?*
- HR strategy / HR admin in headline – *So are you strategic or an administrator?*
- Five different current roles on the profile – *Really?!!*
- Using jargon that only HR professionals have a hope of understanding – *A turn-off for non HR.*
- Targeting SMEs and then using images that represent corporate workplaces – *Incongruent.*
- I versus we versus the team, when you are clearly an independent consultant – *Red flag on authenticity?*

Even if you are meeting in person, your potential client will have checked you out online first. If there is inconsistency they will hesitate or have red flags before they have even met you. Maybe they have seen a bad review online or worse than that – you have been a consultant for years and have no recommendations.

Reviews
An article in the *Harvard Business Review*[4] indicated that it takes just one bad one, two- or three-star review for the probability of buying to fall by 51% on average.

They subsequently went on to buy at a higher value, to avoid any risk.

I have an independently verified feedback company working with our clients to gather feedback and you can also use Google reviews to find out about your clients. The focus is to ensure your clients are delighted by your services. You cannot stop all reviews and the odd lower rating may slip through but if you have a 98% five-star rating it would be easy to see this is out of step with the other reviews, especially if it is anonymous.

YOUR PRESENCE ON SOCIAL MEDIA

The reality is that when people visit your LinkedIn profile or website they are sceptical and will be looking for reasons to trust you before they buy from you, especially if you are in the business to consumer (B2C) marketplace.

To increase your credibility, or as the marketeers call it "social proofing", there are some actions you can take to improve your chances of conversion.

1. Case studies

"More work" I hear you saying. Yes, it's an important element of your credibility. They don't have to be long case studies, more a showcase of the work that you have done, how you did it and the outcomes you have achieved for your client.

If you get into the habit of asking your clients to do case studies as well, you will have a library to choose from in time. If you are new to consulting you can also do case studies on the work you have completed in your current employment – I am sure your employers will be happy to be seen as a progressive organisation in the public's eye. If they are not, then you will need to anonymise it until you have your own clients.

If your client doesn't have time you can always draft a case study for them to review, to speed up the process.

2. Client testimonials

I encourage my clients to provide feedback in several ways (my 360-degree roots aren't far away, even now).

LinkedIn recommendations are important for your credibility. I suggest that any consultant that has a recommendation over three months old is creating a red flag for your potential clients. What does it say? It says either I don't have clients that want to recommend me, or my business processes are such that I am not organised enough to have this as part of my quality process. Now neither of these may be true but buyers are getting choosier.

3. Third party reviews

As mentioned, I use an independent company to gather reviews – a bit like TripAdvisor and Google Reviews – and these are published on my website. You can tailor the questions and showcase other services that you have, allowing you another opportunity to reach out about your services.

I read recently that the average consumer reads 10 third party reviews before they make a purchasing decision.

4. Brand associations

Many years ago, when I focused on business to business (B2B) clients I was very proud to add their logos on my proposals, websites and drop them into every conversation I had. At the time it was BT, Vodafone, the Welsh Assembly Government, Santander, and the list went on. It's only when I reflect now how proud I am that I have influenced, in a small way, some of the best businesses in the UK.

Who do you work with that you can associate with yourself and your business? You do need permission to use logos or you will have their "brand police" on the phone asking you to remove them!

I work with a lot of HR professionals that are transitioning into consulting so it's hard sometimes to get case studies and testimonials until they have "flown the nest". I have five transition stories in Part 5 for you to read. All have been part of my bootcamp programme and whilst they are fairly new to their consulting journey, all have successes to share.

5. Facts and figures

On many websites you will find statistics of how many clients people have, the number of countries they operate in or how many people have read their book or download/s. It can also be a fact about return on investment or some other measurable.

For example I measure in a questionnaire the 5C's, "From Corporate to Consulting" Model at the beginning of our bootcamps and six weeks later.

Some other examples are:

- 100% of our clients increase their confidence, and some double this.
- 100% of our clients increase their clarity.

6. Client content

What's better than your clients talking about you, rather than you talking about yourself?

It's when you see a posting on LinkedIn or Facebook, and you are tagged in it as the person that has helped them on their journey. It's even better when they start using your hashtags as well. Mine are #virtualhrbootcamp and #leapintoconsulting and as these are only relatively new, I need to build up the number of posts using them, as well as encouraging clients to do this too. It will be great to see these hashtags becoming commonly used across my community.

7. Collaborations

My collaborations often share my posts and position my business in front of their clients too. It's a two-way process and reinforces the need to choose the right collaborations.

Content shared by influencers (people that are relevant to your client base that have a high profile and lots of followers) is eight times more likely to get engagement than your own. Share their content across your social media platforms, remembering which platforms are the best for you.

I recently shared a post on LinkedIn from one of the bootcamp students and subsequently got 38,000 views. Think big and intentionally when you are using LinkedIn. Consider the high value relationships that you can build that will create the biggest returns for you both. Make it mutually beneficial.

8. Your website and LinkedIn profile

You have done all the hard work to build your credibility online and then you find that your links on your website or LinkedIn profile don't connect to the right page, or your website has events that took place months ago. It doesn't take much to undermine your presence so a system of updating your media on a regular basis is important.

Equally, do you make it easy for your clients to take action and contact you or buy?

After reviewing over 600 HR consultant LinkedIn profiles in the last five years I found that 70% didn't have a telephone number. The reason for this I discovered was people didn't want to get inundated with potential cold calls from eager salespeople. Let me reassure you that most sales people using LinkedIn would find that approach an inefficient way to get sales; they are more likely to connect with you first and then if they are pushy try and sell to you.

So, if you are in business please make it easy for people to get hold of you.

THE PRESENCE PLATFORM AUDIT

Marketing can seem all-consuming and overwhelming as a consultant and so it's important to assess what you need to focus on and what your priorities are to help you achieve your goals.

Whilst looking at your actions it is also useful to look for your consistency across your platforms. If you change something, have you changed it across all your media? A structured approach to amendments is important and time consuming if you have opted to have a presence on all platforms.

My advice would be to focus on LinkedIn, your website and Facebook, in that order.

LinkedIn is the world's largest live database of professionals. This is where your high value clients can be found and where you can be found.

Your website is your personal shopfront and requires a lot more effort for your site to even rank or become visible to your ideal client. It's all about SEO and a whole range of stats.

Facebook is best used to create community groups and to do targeted Facebook Ads. You no longer have locational restrictions to your business reach. Once you know your ideal client in detail you can use this to target your ads. They are highly effective and good value for money.

This Presence Platform Audit will help you identify what you need to do next. I have also highlighted the key areas to focus on. After all, unless you have a big team of marketeers you won't be able to do all marketing activities – yet!

Presence Platform Audit

Digital Channels	Y/N	Priority for action 1-3	Comments	Next 30 days	Next 60 days	> 3 months
* Website (for your IDEAL client)				☐	☐	☐
Search Engine Optimisation (SEO)				☐	☐	☐
* Google My Business				☐	☐	☐
Google AdWords / pay per click				☐	☐	☐
Remarketing				☐	☐	☐
Videos				☐	☐	☐

Social Media	Y/N	Priority for action 1-3	Comments	Next 30 days	Next 60 days	> 3 months
* Facebook business page				☐	☐	☐
X profile				☐	☐	☐
* LinkedIn personal profile				☐	☐	☐
LinkedIn business profile				☐	☐	☐
Google +				☐	☐	☐
Instagram				☐	☐	☐
YouTube Channel				☐	☐	☐
* Information sharing on social media				☐	☐	☐
* Advertising on social media platforms				☐	☐	☐
* Networking across social media				☐	☐	☐
* Relationship building with influencers				☐	☐	☐
* Using groups to build following				☐	☐	☐
* Activity to push to your website				☐	☐	☐
* Regular postings to all media				☐	☐	☐
* LinkedIn Articles & blogs				☐	☐	☐

Email Marketing	Y/N	Priority for action 1-3	Comments	Next 30 days	Next 60 days	> 3 months
* Customer newsletters				☐	☐	☐
* Prospect newsletters				☐	☐	☐
Marketing funnels				☐	☐	☐
* Regular offers and promotions				☐	☐	☐
* Providing helpful information				☐	☐	☐

Creative Marketing	Y/N	Priority for action 1-3	Comments	Next 30 days	Next 60 days	> 3 months
* Logo used consistently online and offline				☐	☐	☐
* Key messages used on all materials				☐	☐	☐
Necessary collateral, e.g. brochures				☐	☐	☐
Core sales presentation				☐	☐	☐
* Social images and infographics, branded				☐	☐	☐

Traditional Marketing	Y/N	Priority for action 1-3	Comments	Next 30 days	Next 60 days	> 3 months
Printed magazine / newspaper adverts				☐	☐	☐
Printed local guides / advertisers				☐	☐	☐
Flyers				☐	☐	☐
Printed newsletters				☐	☐	☐
Direct marketing (letter to named person)				☐	☐	☐

Face to Face/ Remote	Y/N	Priority for action 1-3	Comments	Next 30 days	Next 60 days	> 3 months
Exhibiting at relevant trade shows / events				☐	☐	☐
Speaking at relevant events				☐	☐	☐

PART 2 || THE "FROM CORPORATE TO CONSULTING" MODEL™

Face to Face/ Remote	Y/N	Priority for action 1-3	Comments	Next 30 days	Next 60 days	> 3 months
Prospect meetings				☐	☐	☐
Existing customer meetings				☐	☐	☐
Partnership relationship meetings				☐	☐	☐
Networking				☐	☐	☐
Hosting events				☐	☐	☐
Peer to peer groups				☐	☐	☐

Public Relations	Y/N	Priority for action 1-3	Comments	Next 30 days	Next 60 days	> 3 months
Press release / editorial				☐	☐	☐
Guest speaker				☐	☐	☐
Advertorials				☐	☐	☐

Other	Y/N	Priority for action 1-3	Comments	Next 30 days	Next 60 days	> 3 months
Telemarketing				☐	☐	☐
Sponsorship				☐	☐	☐
* Resellers & affiliates				☐	☐	☐
* Endorsements / testimonials				☐	☐	☐
Loyalty programmes				☐	☐	☐
Recommend a friend				☐	☐	☐
Branded clothing				☐	☐	☐
Telephone on hold message				☐	☐	☐
* Email signature				☐	☐	☐
* *KEY Priority issues to address*						

YOUR EXPERT POSITIONING

What makes you an expert in your field?

There are lots of people talking about the need to raise your profile so that you are seen to be the expert or the authority. This comes back to the points made in Chapter 10 – Clarity. What would you like to be an expert in?

For many years (and still now occasionally), I was labelled as an expert and authority in designing 360-degree feedback software and programmes. It is true I developed a programme that was leading edge in the UK, providing web-based 360 solutions and a complex system that allowed data gathering and the presentation of the data into a clear and simple report.

This software was later a door opener for my business to be integrated into the UK's leading international psychometrics company. From this I then trained and introduced the product into the key markets in India, Canada, and Europe.

I was the 360 queen!

I was an expert but also, I now had a label, which made it difficult as I felt pigeonholed with some of my clients.

I had built a whole business around this expertise and even this week I have won business to deliver a 360-degree feedback programme for a senior leadership team (20 years after my first 360 project).

As the years have gone by, I have changed the focus of my business and I am now passionate about helping other HR consultants succeed, hence the reason we have this book. That doesn't stop me helping you launch your own products or using my 360 in your portfolio too!

So, once you know what you want to be an expert in how can you continue to develop this? This may be through reading, education, new client work, speaking engagements, and collaborations on related projects?

It is also about your marketing, for example, *I'm the only HR consultant coach in the market to combine over 30 years of HR consulting and the "From Corporate to Consultant" Model.*

This is true because no one else has designed my model! Instantly I am unique.

So, what combinations do you have that can make you unique?

My key area of expertise is: _____

+

My secondary area of expertise is: _____

For example, one of our bootcampers had always been caught between being an accountant and an HR expert. When she revisited her brand recently, we talked about the power of combining the two. It's very powerful for her niche; she works with SMEs and can offer two key professional services.

Once this rebrand took place and the clarity was there the conversations about her services were easier and more successful.

PERSONAL BRANDING

Personal branding offers numerous benefits to a person's life and career. Also, it helps in building confidence while gaining trust, authenticity, and credibility. It is important that you understand what others are doing in your niche. How well a person uses LinkedIn tells you a lot about how serious they are about their personal brand. It is about publishing content, being active and maintaining a robust profile.

It needs revisiting weekly.

Check out the influencers in your niche.

What resonates with their audience?

Check out the speakers at conferences; what are the topics relevant to your niche and what angles are they taking?

_____
_____
_____
_____

What can you do to build on this?

_____
_____
_____
_____

It is also important that you focus on quality not quantity.

Your number one goal is to make your brand discoverable, sharable, and memorable so that it instils trust in anyone you engage with.

You need to stand out from others

Your personal branding right now will be through your presence on Zoom and your social media presence. A picture paints a thousand words, and this is exactly what your photo on social media will say about you. How you show up on Zoom is also important (even if you think it isn't!). When you attend meetings live your brand – but be authentic.

Make the effort!
What does your photo on LinkedIn say about you? Does it elicit a positive response?

According to LinkedIn tips a photo with a smile gets 14 x more views than no photo.

What does the wrong photo say about you? If you are a consultant charging £1000 a day do you look like you are worth it?

It is not about how you look, it's about a professional image

Your photo and brand are your shopfront.

A portrait photo with a smile

Most of the better profiles have smiles – in recent research this was identified as one of the most impactful characteristics of a photo. After all, who wants to work with someone who is negative or miserable? Clients have enough of that anyway!

When clients meet with you, they want to enjoy their time working with you, even if the work is challenging. They want to feel you are on their side.

Your why

We have already touched on your why in Chapter 10 – Clarity.

Your personal branding will be driven by your "why", which you have identified.

The WHY is the purpose, cause, or belief that drives every one of us.

> *"Our WHY is an original story. It is who we are and who we are comes from our past.*
>
> *To find our WHY, we look to the stories, people and experiences that say something about who we are and what we value."*
>
> *Simon Sinek*

Just to recap:

What makes you come alive?

_____
_____

What are your innate strengths?

_____
_____

Where do you add the greatest value?

_____
_____
_____

How will you measure your life?

_____
_____
_____

What legacy do you want to leave?

_____
_____
_____

What have you learnt in your life you would like to pass onto others?

_____
_____
_____

What is your message?

_____
_____
_____

It is your reason for getting out of bed in the morning!

MY WHY

This is my purpose and the meaning I give to my life:

YOUR VALUE

What is your value that you bring to your client?

This is all part of your personal branding.

And remember not to overuse these buzzwords in your copy:

1. Motivated
2. Passionate
3. Creative
4. Driven
5. Expert
6. Track record

Discoverable

So, having established your brand look, you need to be discoverable – not the best kept secret!

Use your real name on social media – not Sarah HG for example (guilty as charged)!

Photo by Adrienn from Pexels

Crosslink your profiles so that all your social media link together easily, including publications.

Raise your profile by blogging and speaking and again, cross-reference with your media profiles.

The technicalities

Now the technical stuff, a whole topic in itself. Your SEO (search engine optimisation) will improve if the file names of anything you post on social media platforms have keywords in them, for example **HR-Consulting-White-Paper.pdf**.

The document is far more likely to be discoverable in searches this way. So, you may need to rename some of your already existing content.

Current content file name	SEO-friendly rename

Visit https://leap-into-consulting.mykajabi.com/products/book-downloads for a downloadable version of this.

Social media links

Add your social media channels to all touch points:

Email signatures – linked to social media

PowerPoint Presentations – an example final slide – all with embedded links

Out of office messages – add what you are doing – links and content

For example, if you are out of the office and speaking at the CIPD Festival of Work, add in when you are speaking and a link to your online information.

You could also add a link to the presentation. It is all about giving value and raising your discoverability.

On this basis it makes good sense to use your out of office more frequently and in an intentional way.

Thought leaders

If you want to be involved in speaking at conferences and events you can add a page to your website – maybe a banner with an image of you in action?

Many consultants want to be thought leaders in their niche – and to do this you need to listen to what is happening around you to notice what is important.

Recently I was approached by *People Management*, one of the HR industry leading magazines, to add comment to a topic being published. You will only get approached to do this if you have a presence and actively comment on news items or you have paid a PR agency!

Identify who you see as the thought leaders in your niche currently. See what they are talking about, where they hang out and what their brand is like.

And then be different!
Hone your listening skills and be inquisitive. Ask lots of questions and find out more about your niche. Take a real interest. If you are struggling to do this naturally then it might indicate that you are not in the right niche. If you are not passionate about it then revisit your why and niche.

With all aspects of personal branding it is about instilling trust and confidence in your potential clients.

Make your brand stand out – always!
Mine is centred around the colour turquoise and Greece – and I am unwavering in this. My branding and my personal style all match! As I said a little earlier, if you were to ask anyone what comes to mind when they think of me one of the top answers would be turquoise!

I have recently rebranded the Leap into Consulting® services and products to reflect my ideal clients. The new look is fresh, modern and of course fifty shades of blue.

MAXIMISING YOUR SOCIAL MEDIA PRESENCE

Social media is forever evolving and as soon as this book is published some of this advice will be out of date.

The current platforms I recommend to build your brand and expert positioning are LinkedIn and Facebook Adverts. For both platforms you will need to have a business page.

The reason for this is that the functionality varies between your personal page and your company page. If you focus your attention though it must be on your personal brand. After all, people buy people.

I run regular webinars for LinkedIn which you are welcome to join, and we cover social media in more detail on our bootcamps.

The link to join the webinar "How to Superboost Your Consulting Profile" can be found on our resources page at the end of the book.

MARKET RESEARCH

"I'm only a solopreneur. Surely I don't need to do market research?"

Well it's important to understand your marketplace and the trends that are taking place. As an HR consultant it's critical to be commercially savvy.

What I mean by this is:

Understand your clients

Take an interest in the clients that you have – beyond the project that you are working on. Be inquisitive; ask questions and meet people across the business to broaden your visibility.

I have also learnt over the years, sometimes the hard way, that not all clients are good clients.

If a client is a time vampire and you are not asking for the right fees you are depriving your other "right" clients of your valuable services.

Again, many of my clients that are new to consulting would rather have some paying clients than none, and I do understand this. However as soon as it is possible re-evaluate the clients you have. If it's not working for you, it probably isn't working for them either.

Understand your marketplace

Know what is trending and be up to date with what is happening. Better still, create the trending thought content. Don't be afraid to put across your point of view. Controversy creates interest.

This week three of my clients were trending on LinkedIn for the first time. This is so exciting and is great feedback that your content is reaching the right people and creating engagement.

Understand your competitors

And if you don't know who your competitors are then research is needed to find out. This is so easy with the internet search functions.

You can find most of your answers just using these platforms:

- Google Trends
- LinkedIn Insights

Remember not to compare apples with pears on this one. You may be one of three HR consultants in your local Chamber of Commerce but are you all the same? I doubt it very much. You all have your own uniqueness.

A wise business colleague said to me that you will attract the right tribe for you. We all have different values and personalities and we end up working with the right people for us.

AWARDS

Early years

I often joke about the awards season in the business world and to a degree I am cynical about the motives behind some of these. Most have a commercially focused bias with the benefits to the award winners and sponsors being secondary.

I was not blessed with awards as a child and it was a rare moment if I gained a certificate or accolade. I wasn't sporty, not gifted academically (even though I worked hard), and although I would have loved to have awards, I resigned myself to the fact that these were for other people.

Business awards

In my business career life has been different. I was one of the first businesses in Hertfordshire to gain the Investors in People award in record time (three months) and then there was a long dry spell, because I hadn't given them any importance, until 2014 and more recently a string of awards since 2018:

- Influential Small Business Owner – 2018
- CIPD Finalist Best HR Consultancy – 2018
- Business & Industry Today – HR Consultancy of the Year – 2020
- South Women in Business – Finalist – Business Reinvention Award 2020
- Finalist HR Business Book of the Year - 2021
- Top 30 Most Influential HR Thinker – 2024
- Finalist SME Businesswoman of the Year - 2024

I have either entered for these awards or have been nominated and what I have learnt is that whilst it might take time to complete the various stages of the award process, the feeling you get when you win or are recognised as a finalist amongst your peer group (and family) is emotional. I have learnt to wear waterproof mascara.

If you are thinking to yourself that you haven't done anything to deserve an award, just reflect on the impact of the work that you are doing for your clients. In there will be some golden nuggets that you can share and show the influence and results you get.

I entered the All-Star Marketing Awards for Influential Small Business Owner because I was persuaded to by the directors – I didn't think my work was a worthy story. Then I started to put together the details and realised that I had created an ROI of 435% and saved the charity over £60,000 in three months. The external panel of judges also recognised this, and this is how I won that award.

My partner and one of my sons were with me at the event and I was so shocked that I cried – hence the red face if you ever see any photos of the event online.

Awards do build credibility and I would urge you to apply for the ones that are relevant to you, your business, and your story.

We have now created The HR Consultancy Academy Awards® dedicated to the profession of HR & People Consulting and related support functions. These Awards take place annually at our HR Consultancy Academy Festival.

What awards would you like to win in the next five years?

Reflection

Action points

Chapter 12:
Collaboration

Collaboration is when a group of people come together and contribute their expertise for the benefit of a shared objective, project, or mission.

As a consultant in your early years collaborating with others will create better problem solving, new learning opportunities, a larger team of experts to work with, and it's great for mutual support. Here are some other benefits of collaboration.

It's fun and it speeds up your results

The sad thing is that you could find it overwhelmingly hard work setting up your own business – you could find it so difficult that you could find it more attractive to go back into corporate life. I have seen clients wavering with this thought during their early years as a consultant. For the extroverts amongst us we are energised by being with other people on a regular basis. The current use of technology to collaborate just doesn't do it for many people, even though it is a very efficient way to communicate and build relationships with potential and existing clients.

Having people you can bounce ideas off and work with is essential for your growth, and your business.

It's not lonely

If you try and do it alone it is likely to be slow, hard work and lonely. It may feel a slog, you may feel that you are not enjoying it, and ultimately you may give up.

The topic of community was mentioned by a client of mine in a recent review:

> **HR Consulting Bootcamp**
> "I thought being a consultant would be lonely, and I wouldn't have much support, but I actually feel more connected and supported by this group than my own current employer." Anon

We spend time on the topic of Collaboration as a module on the Virtual Bootcamp because it shows you can **generate income faster** and easier – because when you are working in collaboration with the **right partners you move faster and generate additional income more easily** because it's not just you having to do it on your own.

WORKING WITH PARTNERS

In addition to product partners you will meet people both online and at events and networking meetings that you strike up a relationship with where you can add value to each other's businesses.

They may be solicitors, accountants or other providers of products or services that are complementary to you.

I have worked closely with a small handful of people whom I trust and whose opinion I value. We are aware of what we can offer clients and where we can, and if appropriate, we refer clients to each other.

Often you will find some of your collaborations will be one-way streets and this is when it's best to meet and just review what else needs to happen for them to create more opportunities for you.

There are so many HR related products that exist in the marketplace that these companies are keen for you to introduce them to your clients. Many of these companies have referral schemes and provide fantastic products and services that can expand your portfolio from Day 1. Once you have defined the services that you want to offer your clients then you will be able to find products to add to your portfolio.

As a consulting business I have developed partnerships covering these areas:

- Psychometric testing
- Employee engagement surveys
- Recruitment (ATS) – applicant tracking system
- HRIS (HR information system)
- Candidate vetting services
- Online training portals

As part of being a partner I look at the reliability of the services, the support they give partners and the credibility of the solution in the marketplace. I actively search out new solutions to ensure that I am ahead of many other consultants.

If you worry about the transition from employed to going self-employed this is a great way to bridge the gap and start your referral income as well as getting up to speed.

This will give you great opportunities for door-opening conversations with your clients and will accelerate you getting new clients.

What makes a great collaboration/partner for you?

We are all different in terms of what works for us but for me these are some of the aspects I have learnt are useful:

- Do they have a great product or service that your clients will love – and it will add value to their business?
- What is the reliability of the product (if technology based)?
- Where are the servers based (GDPR)?
- Does the company have marketing support materials you can white label (brand for yourself)?
- Is the partner happy to promote your services to their database?
- Are the ethos and values of the company aligned with yours?
- Is there a clear partnership agreement in place?
- Is the energy and time you spend getting up to speed commercially viable for you?
- Are the commercial aspects of the relationship favourable for you and your clients?

Who are your perfect partners?

You are unlikely to have time to be an expert in many products so I would suggest starting with the two that will be your best door openers.

Revisit your ideal client – what problems do they have that could be solved with one of these new products?

For example, BreatheHR is a software solution for SMEs – it provides a professional cloud-based platform that can benefit your SME clients by:

- Engaging remote workers
- Giving immediate access to all employees' data (admin users)
- Helping line managers manage their teams well
- Allowing you as the consultant to be able to advise remotely
- Building trust and openness as data is available to the employee

And the list goes on.

For your SME clients this is a great solution; it's good value for them and easy for you to set up and manage and it also creates great return on investment (ROI).

Many consultants embed these systems into their retainer package which extends the life of their relationship beyond a one-off project. By adding value on an ongoing basis, creating reports on absence, performance, and other measures it allows you to have strategic conversations.

What products or services would you like to add to your business?
The quickest way to find products is to attend exhibitions as it's free to enter and you can accelerate your understanding of what is available and what new products are on the market. It's good to have unique products rather than be part of the crowd. Many exhibitions are now online as well so it's easy to see what's new as well as the tried and tested options.

Maximise the relationship

To get the most from your partnerships I highly recommend attending relevant training, webinars and actively being involved in your partners' Facebook and LinkedIn groups. This is where many of your potential clients can be found.

In my experience the closer the collaborations you have, the better the support you get and it works well.

A note of caution

Be clear about who provides your client with support. Is it technical support or client support? Are you set up to take the volume of calls that might happen when you implement new software?

The boundaries need to be in your terms and conditions and if you are offering admin support this will need to be costed into the proposal at a lower rate – keep your fees for the high value work and your client will appreciate this.

Here are some of the benefits from working with product partners:
- Working with dynamic product owners and entrepreneurs
- A source of inspirational guest speakers for your events
- Joint ventures and projects with their clients
- Scale-up of your business
- Peer group for support (beyond the product)
- Increased revenue, over and above your consulting income
- Increased profit (because it's technology based)
- Increased credibility amongst your clients
- Great door openers for your clients
- Greater impact on solving your clients' problems
- Ability to add objectivity into your services by providing data and stats

What proof have I got that this works?

Not that I need to convince you, but I am sure you would like to know some of the success stories, so here are two.

Employee engagement
This example both supports the use of LinkedIn to keep in touch and build relationships as well as collaborating with partners. It involved a client that I

had worked with over a number of years and who had since moved on to a new organisation.

I had lost touch for whatever reason. One day his LinkedIn profile popped up and I was inquisitive to see what was happening in his world. I private messaged him with nothing more than "hope all is well in your world".

This started the dialogue that ended with a proposal for an employee engagement system and consulting support for two years.

It solved a problem that he had with engagement and we could provide valuable insights into what was happening across his organisation both in terms of engagement and leadership.

The value of this contract was around £40k and launched us into the space of employee engagement programmes. Without our collaboration with our employee engagement partner this would not have been possible.

HRIS

Faced with setting up a new business from scratch in 2015, I needed to accelerate my growth and connection to SMEs in Dorset and Hampshire.

Anyone that has ever worked with SMEs will know that engaging with HR solutions can sometimes be difficult unless you have a solution to a problem, as I have already talked about in Chapter 10 – Clarity.

What was the problem I was solving with a cloud-based HR system?
Many small businesses have no dedicated HR function and if they are lucky someone wears the "HR hat" as part of another role, usually office management, finance, or payroll.

- The burden on small businesses is high in terms of HR admin and you can guarantee as a business owner or managing director they often needed information off site, locked away in a filing cabinet in the office – with the owner of the key not available.

- People management activities were often done out of hours, including performance reviews (even in enlightened businesses).
- There was also a sense that absence levels were high, but there was no real tracking in place.
- On top of this holiday management was a long winded and complex problem, often involving wall charts and numerous excel spreadsheets.

The solution
The implementation of a cloud-based HR technology system including a full audit on HR administration and documents and setting up and training staff.

The results for clients
- This resulted in fully accessible data, anywhere, anytime not just for managers but staff as well.
- It was GDPR compliant and removed the need for paper-based copies, freeing up space and allowing for an audit to be done on what paperwork was required and what had "expired".
- An added benefit in many clients was the connectivity across multiple sites and the engagement through the various functions on the system to build relationships with people that were field based.
- The investment in one of my largest clients was an ROI of 435%, and the organisation employed 350 staff, so the implementation cost was higher than normal.
- There were higher levels of professionalism when recruiting and onboarding new staff.

The results for my business
- Accelerated growth of client base and income streams.
- The ability to manage all clients remotely, on one dashboard.
- The creation of long-term relationships that lent itself to retainers.

There are many more, but I would love to hear your stories for my next edition of this book!

WORKING WITH ASSOCIATES

When it goes well

Having a team of associates can be useful for the bigger projects that you run or for areas of expertise that you may not have. Also, you may have grown to the point where you need other people to deliver your projects, whilst you manage the business.

Choosing the right associates is an art but given you are likely to be skilled at recruitment this may not be a problem for you.

Ignore the fact they are associates and treat the process of recruitment as seriously, or more seriously than you would for an employee. The aim is to find people that you can trust fully and have a similar outlook to you, that live your values and will fly the flag for your brand and business.

Start looking for associates from Day 1, even if you don't have work available. You need to start building the relationship and have an associate agreement in place before you may need them. Being proactive is important as you never know when that large project will land on your doorstep.

First, I would recommend working with them on a piece of work that you can delegate that doesn't go directly to a client and then reviewing this.

- How much management did they need?
- What is the quality of their work?
- Is it delivered on time?
- How flexible are they with their time?
- How professional are they?

One of my largest projects involved a team of six consultants working for a period of three months. It was important to have consistency and the team really enjoyed the work and collaboration. I was able to leave the team to deliver this important project – they were a great team and very professional.

When it really doesn't go well

It doesn't always go this well and over the years I have found that there is a temptation that an associate will try and seduce the client away from your business to work with them. I will give you an example.

In 2009, I was running an award-winning programme with a client I had worked with for 10 years. It was the year my father was diagnosed with cancer and I brought in an associate to support running the events with me, at my cost, in case I needed to leave to be with him.

Sure enough I needed to call on her to step in, which of course she was more than happy to do.

When it came to the tendering process later that year at which I was due to present my new revised programme for 2010, in fact the morning my dad died, I met the client on the way up to the family in Worcestershire. I am not sure how to this day I kept it all together at that meeting, but I did.

I found out a couple of weeks later that I wasn't awarded the new contract.

Funnily enough my associate had pitched for the work and despite an associate agreement in place preventing her from doing this the client worked with her, using all my intellectual property and knowledge. She went on to deliver this for several years and I did contemplate suing her for the value of the programme (which was substantial), and breach of contract.

But grief is a strange thing; it makes you reflect on what is important in your life, and this client with a set of values and morals completely misaligned with mine and an associate that took advantage of a very difficult time in my life, were well matched.

I walked away because I could see the bigger picture.

What have I learnt from working with associates?

Key relationship
I have learned a lot from working with associates. I have learnt new skills, new perspectives and enjoyed the collaborations from work that we have done together. I wouldn't want the above story to put you off; it is fair to say but what I have learned is that you must retain the key relationship with your clients. Whilst you can delegate elements of the project the reviews and the sponsor for the client project must remain with you.

Priorities
As associates work for several different companies and clients, they will always have priorities for the work that they are currently delivering. The better the relationship you have with your associates the more likely they are to prioritise you over their other clients. As part of this process they are likely to look at how quickly you pay your invoices and the volume of work that you will pass their way. A key factor will also be the type of work that you deliver to clients and how that fits in with their expertise. Ultimately, it's all about trust and the relationship that you both have. I always look for win–win scenarios.

Working with friends
Often when I'm talking to people that are setting up their consulting businesses, they talk to me about going into partnership or having an associate that's their friend join them. The question I would ask you, if this is on your radar, is do you value your friendship more than you do their commercial relationship with your business? Unless your friendship is extremely robust the chances are that something may happen in the future that will upset this relationship. I have had this happen to me too and it took over 12 months for that relationship to repair itself after I stopped working with that individual. Maybe it's worth trialling it on a short-term basis to see how it works and agreeing what will happen in certain scenarios. It's almost like having a prenuptial agreement.

Working with professional service partners

Many progressive professional service firms are looking to broaden their portfolio of services for their clients. Accountants, payroll providers, and law firms are good partners for your HR business.

Again, be passionate about the services they offer too. Do you use their services? Do you refer people to them? Do they in turn make referrals to you?

I have an informal partnership with a local law firm in Dorset and my accountant in Hampshire. I happily refer clients to them and with both partners we have created new joint services over the years.

Some of the collaborative events that I have run with partners:

1. *A workshop* on "The integration of cultures after a merger or acquisition", with a leading accounting firm.

2. A group called the **HR Advantage Group** for standalone HR professionals to meet with peers monthly and learn about business law for HR professionals. This was run in conjunction with a local law firm.

3. *Retreat income generator events* where my product partners are invited to speak to my audience of HR consultants to accelerate their business growth.

4. *Exhibition stands at Olympia and Excel* where partners have joined to support and showcase their services as well.

5. *Webinars on a range of topics*, one most recently on pivoting your business in turbulent economic conditions with an accountant.

Who do you know that you could partner with?

You may find the downloadable worksheet (from https://leap-into-consulting.mykajabi.com/products/book-downloads) useful when brainstorming this activity.

Collaboration		
Associates	**Product / Service Partners**	**Business Support**
What?	What?	What?
Who?	Who?	Who?
How?	How?	How?

Reflection

Action points

Chapter 13:
Courage

Once you have completed the previous four stages of the model taking action and having courage is the biggest challenge, though following through may also be a challenge for you. This depends on how busy you are, what systems and methodologies you have in place and the support you have around you. It will also be influenced by your personality and your preference for working with detail and structure.

I have mentioned before about profiling and one tool I use measures the four factors of the DISC model. You will find lots of information about the background to this on the internet. Here I point out how one of those factors (although they are never in isolation) may impact on how you manage your business.

In the DISC model, the "C" relates to compliance and depending on where you are on the scale you will get an indication of your preferences to working in a structured manner and with attention to detail. If you have a high score you are likely to prefer creating structures, lists, methodologies and a way of working. If you have a low score you are likely to seek new way of doing things and may not have the structured approach that other "high C"s enjoy.

Even if a "high C" isn't your preference it doesn't mean to say you can't do it, but in my case where I know I enjoy structure and also flexibility, I need to have systems to help keep me efficient and focused without feeling it's overly complex.

One of my coaches once shared with me some research that indicated that 84% of delegates do not follow through from what they have learnt on an event.

Being motivated, being driven, and wanting something to change is not enough – what makes the difference in taking action is **accountability.**

So, you need to have a plan that is going to make you tackle action if you want to get to six figures. You are likely to be outside your comfort zone at times, however it's the key to accelerating your success.

You need courage to take action, to pick up the phone. Because **without action you are unlikely to succeed.** At the end of the day your willingness to do this is what will make this work for you. And the thing that most people avoid is taking the sort of action that brings results.

> *"Accountability breeds responsibility."*
> S Covey

I attended Action Coach meetings for a short while and one of the models I remember them sharing was this. I believe it is a Brad Sugars model. It says that,

"In order to HAVE anything in life, we need to DO something to achieve it, and in order to DO the right things in the right way at the right time, we have to BE the right person ... which means BE X DO = HAVE".

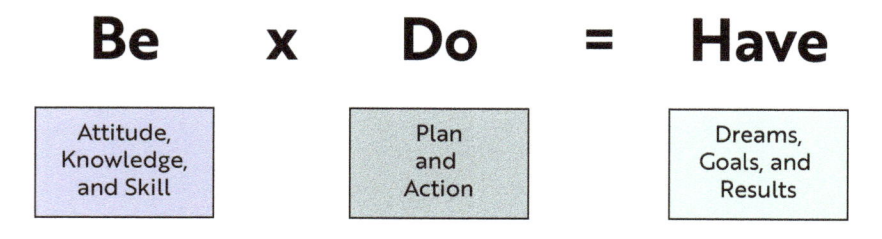

Be x Do = Have

| Attitude, Knowledge, and Skill | Plan and Action | Dreams, Goals, and Results |

Taking action as I have said is important and so too is taking the right actions and having effective work habits.

In this next section we go through tips and techniques for helping you take action.

"Motivation is what gets you started - habits are what keep you going"

EFFECTIVE WORK HABITS

Running your own business is tough. It means being motivated, efficient, and persistent. When you are responsible for all of this it can be challenging. So, you need to work smarter not harder, so that all the important stuff gets done.

Laying the foundations

1. Clear direction
2. Understanding your why
3. Lasting change
4. The slight edge

To be successful, you must understand what success looks like for you. It means different things to different people. You need to be clear for you, what are you trying to achieve? Once you understand where you are going it is much easier to plan the route. You will have explored this in the Confidence and Clarity chapters.

You may remember reading Alice in Wonderland as a child. Alice arrives at a fork in the road and sees the Cheshire cat in the tree and asks, *"Which road do I take?"* He asks Alice, *"Where do you want to go?"* *"I don't know,"* Alice responds. Then said the cat, *"It doesn't matter."*

All success is goal-directed action, so that everything you do is aimed at achieving those goals, both personal and business life. You have already reviewed this as part of your Wheel of Life in Chapter 9 – Confidence.

We have already talked about finding your why in Chapter 10 – Clarity. There are lots of different reasons for what it is that makes you wake up and work towards your goals. If you don't know your why it probably means your goals are not clearly aligned. Your why is what keeps you motivated.

To be successful you need to be motivated and to be motivated you must understand what your success looks like and what you need to do to get there. Once you have your goals you are motivated to work towards them and when you achieve that success, you are then motivated to do it again. It's a circle of reinforcement.

> *"If you are not making the progress you would like to make, and are capable of making, it is simply because your goals are not clearly defined."*
> Paul J Meyer

Within reason you can achieve whatever you want. With the steps that you need to take, get clear and specific in what you need to do to achieve your goals. Think big and work towards your goals every day.

If you don't have clear goals and a strategy to get there you run the risk of being distracted. In the absence of clearly defined goals, you can become strangely loyal to performing daily acts of trivia. You may hop onto LinkedIn or Facebook or be distracted by emails.

You need to be clear daily on how you are going to achieve those goals for the day.

How can we create lasting change?

We need to achieve success and results, so what behaviours do we need to adopt to achieve those results?

To change any behaviours that don't serve you well, you need to adopt a positive attitude and create habits that get you to do actions that create your success.

If we can find small habits in our business that create business success this will create lasting success. It's repetition, doing it over and over again – it's doing new habits. And if something isn't working, we have to go back to that behaviour and see what works and what doesn't and learn from it.

Not everyone gets out of bed every day motivated. So those habits we can then rely on will get us through the day and then when we achieve success, even when it is a small step, we will do it all again.

You might think that you must make massive changes to your business to be successful, but you can make big changes by tweaking things by a small amount.

> *"We didn't improve one thing by 100%, we improved 100 things by 1%."*
> *Sir Clive Woodward*

The exponential results can be amazing so it is worth thinking about all areas of your business and working habits and deciding on a small improvement you can make in each area, such as:

- Change supplier
- Reduce expenses
- Get better processes
- Use time more effectively

When you are running a business it is your responsibility, 100%, all of the time so you need to work effectively and efficiently. Effectively means doing the right things, and efficiently means doing them right, first time every time – aim for this. Your personal responsibility is to do the right things the right way and in the right priority order. This includes your team.

Sometimes we get so caught up in the doing, instead of communicating and delegating. Goals go out of the window because we are so busy doing stuff.

How does this make us feel? Working like that is stressful and not sustainable and we really need to think about what we do daily.

This brings us to the combination of urgent versus important.

How do you react in these situations?

> *Urgent and important* – These are for example staff matters such as the suspension of a member of staff, and preparing reports.

> *Important but not urgent* – This is more proactive: can we plan in time in the diary now before it becomes urgent and stressful? For example, there is no such thing as an urgent email. If it is that important, they will phone you and if they put "Urgent" in the subject line this is their priority not yours. Don't get distracted from your important work.

> *Urgent not important* – This includes interruptions from others, pointless activities, or routines.

> *Not urgent and not important* – This might be social media, Facebook, going to the gym, having a meal with friends. We spend so much time in this box (the stress box). We just need five minutes out to destress – but that then drifts into longer. If we spend more time in proactive mode, we will need less time in the "escape" box and then we can have a reward instead.

When we are much more proactive, we are going to set goals at all levels and schedule these in our daily diary and communicate this to the people who need to know. Then we can start working on these tasks.

Do planning first before leaping into the doing, and of course review what went well and what you have learnt. It's calmer and you get far more done. The key to all of this is proper planning – it can save you time. For every minute you spend planning you save 10 X in executing.

Finding 10 minutes per day is the equivalent to 22 workdays. What could you do with this extra time that you have saved? What could you do with an extra hour a day – that's two extra months a year?

When we are interrupted it takes us 20 minutes to get back into the zone. This includes every interruption, so looking at emails and texts etc.

Just three interruptions a day means one hour of lost productivity.

Set time aside that is uninterrupted to focus on that one thing. Be clear you can't be interrupted during this time. An hour of uninterrupted time is four times more productive than broken time so even 10 minutes' planning at the beginning of the day or at the end of the day can have a massive impact on your day.

We know that we must have clearly defined goals. I talked about dreaming big in Chapter 9 – Confidence.

How can we then break these down into a list of goals, monthly goals, weekly goals, and then the daily goals and habits?

SMART goals

"The trouble with not having a goal is that you can spend your life running up and down the field and never score."
Bill Copeland

We have been brought up in a world where the acronym SMART is used in all aspects of education and work. It is widely used, but attributable to George Doran in 1981 and was developed to enable managers to achieve their business goals.

A quick reminder of what it stands for:

Your goals always need to be **SMART**:

> **S**pecific
> **M**easurable
> **A**chievable
> **R**ealistic
> **T**imebound

By articulating your goals in writing it is more powerful than having them in your head. Whatever works for you, maybe write them down in your plans and diary, and write them on a vision board or a whiteboard. I have my goals clearly written on the whiteboard in the office.

Brainstorm also what might stop you from achieving these and what you can do to overcome any barriers. It helps to share your goals and be held accountable for them. Coaches even need coaches and I have more than one, depending on the needs at the time!

Are you a list maker?

The problem with lists is you may not prioritise against importance and urgency.

Choose one key item you want to complete, with a couple of other smaller goals. Allocate the amount of time you think this will take. Do you have enough time in your diary? If not, you may need to delegate it or agree to change a goal delivery for something else. If it is a client then give them plenty of notice that you cannot meet the previously agreed deadline.

Use a methodology

You may have your own methodology; I prefer the Action Day Diary which is designed for you to achieve your goals and keep focused. And yes, it's a hard copy old fashioned diary!

Prioritise time for your important work and then add in time for other work, if you have availability.

Add in wiggle room of an hour per day, in case clients have an emergency. If this isn't used, then you can decide how best to use this time instead.

Block out chunks of time for calls and emails so that you are focused and not distracted. Thirty minutes in the morning for ad hoc calls and two chunks of time for emails is plenty. If you don't do this, you will create a work pattern that is dictated to you by ad hoc and reactive work. It's easy to get to the end of the day and feel proud that you have answered all your emails and calls to then find your high value work hasn't been delivered.

The key is to do at least 15 minutes of planning a day.

> *"Today isn't over until tomorrow is planned."*

Avoid rollercoasters

Consistently blocking out time in your diary for social media and relationship building is important to avoid the rollercoaster ride that will come from sporadic activity.

Too busy to do this? Guess what? You will finish your current projects that have kept you so busy to find you have no future work lined up, which makes it no better than the world of contracting. You will then be under pressure to find and convert sales. Clients can sense when you are under pressure to sell. You will come across as desperate – and even start discounting your price to get a client on board.

Little and often wins, or when you have the resources recruit additional people to your team to support you so that you focus on the added value work. The other option is to automate as much as you can.

Create efficiency and systems
Automate social media and all other systems where you can so that progress can happen even when you are busy. However, my recommendation is to top and tail your week to be in your office on Monday and Friday. Three days out delivering work per week is about as much as is possible without quality being impacted. With the current working from home this will make it even more efficient and easier to do.

When I was delivering consulting projects, I used to use my Monday to get everything finalised for the week and to work on the business. It was also our team briefing day.

Friday was the following up day from all the work or business development that had taken place during the week. Writing new proposals for clients takes time, until you have a bank of them to draw from.

Follow-up is important for your clients and shows you are organised and proactive. Being on the back foot with delivery of work is a sure way of upsetting your clients and they will be reluctant to work with you again.

Getting a PA/VA (virtual assistant) lined up is key to freeing up your time. Build a relationship now, and delegate your lower value tasks so that you can be freed up to earn your high value fees. This will accelerate your growth and efficiency.

> *"A decision without action is the beginning of delusion."*
> Michael Bernoff

TAKING THE RIGHT ACTIONS

Unless you are taking the right actions and do it consistently you are unlikely to get results. This may lead to disappointment and you could even begin to think this isn't for you. Maybe you don't have the consultant's DNA. Maybe you will go back to the corporate world that you were so keen to leave?

So how do you know what the right actions are?

It depends what your problems are in your business. Most business owners when starting focus on the commercial side of the business, especially on sales and personal income. Looking at metrics can be useful to keep you on track.

Effective business stats
Some of these stats may not be relevant in your first few months but they are certainly useful to know for your planning in the future.

- How long does it take to convert a client?
- What is the average spend of your client?
- What are your most profitable services/products?
- What is the average lifetime of a client?

The more you know about these stats the easier it is to do your business forecasting.

Snapshot of forecasting income
I use stats from my CRM system to measure some of these easily, but it is also easy to start with to calculate these from spreadsheets too:

$$\text{\# of leads you have} \times \text{Your conversion rate (\%)} = \text{\# of predicted customers}$$

Working out how many potential clients you need to talk to a week, to hit your sales target, is a revelation. As your conversation rates increase with experience the volume of people you need to connect with will reduce. You will also have your existing clients to nurture as well.

$$\text{\# of customers} \times \text{\# of transactions per year} \times \text{Average sale price} = \text{Projected revenue (£) per annum}$$

By calculating this you will know how much you need to scale up your relationship building activities and also if you have a large number of leads and they are not converting this can allow you to explore why they are not converting. Is it your package, pricing or maybe you are not yet skilled enough in marketing and selling your services to your clients?

This equation can be used in different ways – maybe you know how much profit you want to make and the percentage margins? You can then work backwards to see how much income you need to generate.

The key is always to focus on profit.

$$\text{Revenue} \times \text{Profit margin (\%)} = \text{Profit (£)}$$

The more you track these stats the more accurately you will be able to predict your income and profit as an independent consultant. As you grow your business beyond yourself to a team of employed staff and/or associates you will need a more sophisticated strategy for your business planning and financing.

Effective progress measures

These are the main areas to review for your business and any good software package will be able to give you this information at the press of a button.

The key is to review this and make appropriate decisions:

- Weekly cash flow forecast
- Aged debtors and creditors
- KPIs
- Monthly P&L
- Quarterly balance sheet

If you have a mentor or accountant working with you, you can review and plan each quarter.

Break big projects down into staged payments and ensure your invoicing is done on time, setting up automated reminders for outstanding invoices. Your payment terms need to be clear including information about interest payments and penalties for late payment. If you experience financial difficulties in your business or personal life don't bury your head in the sand as there are many options out there you can turn to for help.

Break-even point

This is a key figure to calculate. What income do you need to generate before you can make a profit?

> Break even = Overheads (fixed & variable) ÷ Gross profit margin %
> Gross profit margin (%) = Gross margin/Revenue
> Gross margin = Revenue – Variable costs

Your KPIs and business goals

Finance is only one of your KPIs and you will want to create your own "dashboard". Remember the Wheel of Life from Chapter 9 – Confidence. You can also create a business Wheel of Life with your KPIs on it. Keep it balanced, as finance is only one aspect. Other areas that typically are measured include:

- % of billable time
- Customer ratings
- Staff turnover
- Number of new clients

Originating from the US Army in the 1960s is the acronym:

KISS

Keep it Simple and Straightforward

Don't create metrics and KPIs that overcomplicate your life and whose value is disproportionate to the time you put into measuring them.

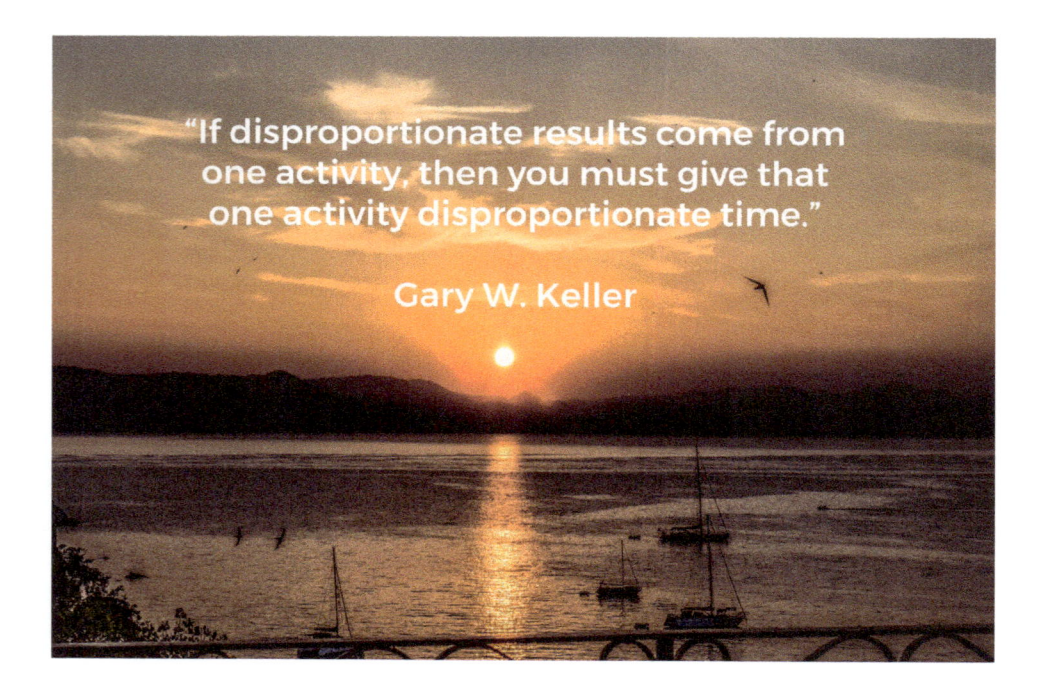

> "If disproportionate results come from one activity, then you must give that one activity disproportionate time."
>
> Gary W. Keller

GIVING IT ALL AWAY

"If you can reduce the price of this project, I am sure we will have lots of other future work for you."

A great author and someone that I admire greatly for starting me on my journey to writing this book is Vishal Morjaria. I remember our first Wow Bookcamp where he talked about the principles of a fair exchange.

If I provide you with an excellent service that creates value for you, is it a fair exchange for receiving the appropriate pay? Of course, you will say yes but this doesn't seem to happen when you go into consulting and are beginning your journey. When I speak to new independent consultants, they have mastered the art of giving away their services, products, and time for either nothing or below cost.

This is because your potential clients have also mastered the art of promising you that this "quick question" or "have you got a template I can use" will lead to bigger and better work.

You must value yourself and your services from Day 1, be ruthlessly focused on how you spend your time, and delegate wherever possible. You are your greatest asset, so spending one hour creating a document (which probably isn't your skillset) is better spent earning 10 X in fee earning activities.

Remember you may be Day 1 as a consultant, but you haven't just started as an HR professional so charge your time out accordingly.

Not charging for your time accurately – "it's only a quick phone call"

How many solicitors do you know that you can just phone up and get advice for free of charge? Not many, I guess? So how will your structure your business so that the numerous "I thought I would give you a quick ring for your advice" calls from friends, family, and clients are handled in a way that ensures you maintain the right level of fees?

One area that solicitors have down to a fine art is the tracking of every six minutes of their time. I'm not suggesting for one minute that you do the same but measuring your time to start with is important. If you are using finance software, you will find that most have functionality to track time spend on projects or clients. This can easily be converted into an invoice. Even if you are not billing your clients by the hour, or part of, it is good practice to log this anyway. You may find that this gives you a greater level of accuracy when quoting for retainer work.

You must have targets on the fees that you need to achieve to create the income that you have set yourself. Once you have identified what you want to earn in your first year this can be broken down into the number of fee-earning hours you need to do per week or month. You will have done this already as part of Chapter 10 – Clarity.

Start with tight boundaries and your clients will respect your time from Day 1. It is more difficult to go back to a client three years down the line and start billing them for time spent on the phone that used to be "part of the service" or in many cases free!

And remember there are great project tracking apps that I recommend as part of your finance software that are aimed at small businesses and will save you time and ensure you have the detail that you need to analyse your business and your time and provide your client with project summaries at a glance.

"Cash is king"

Your current income may be very reliable, consistent, and significant in your corporate role: monthly payments on the same day and typically for the same amount. This creates a huge amount of security for you to plan your life.

Cash flow is king as a business owner, and I advise that large projects are broken down into staged payments and that an initial deposit is paid. Start as you mean to go on and if possible, get a member of your team to do the credit chasing so that you can remain focused on the programme delivery. Using a cloud-based system will be essential for being efficient and professional. When you set it up the system will send out automated reminders and you can also set up payment options for people to pay directly into your bank.

Step into the world of consulting or any other business and suddenly you find yourself in a new cycle of finance. You may be holding back from moving into consulting because of the perceived lack of financial stability or you simply don't want to take the risk. There is one huge advantage of being a consultant and that is you are in control of your own destiny. The first few months may be more challenging but when your business is up and running you will regain your sense of security.

I understand more than anyone what it is like to have commitments and of course if you are a single parent or newly redundant you will want to be sure to be able to provide stability and consistency for your family.

> "Invest in yourself. Your career is the engine of your wealth."
> PAUL CLITHEROE

However, I am also surprised at the number of professional women that I talk to that want sign-off from their husbands before deciding on joining one of our programmes. This often leads to disappointment because their husbands/partners don't buy into their vision for being self-employed, or challenge the investment in coaching and development.

Interestingly I have never heard a man say, "I'll just check this with my wife."

> THE BEST WAY TO PREDICT THE FUTURE IS TO CREATE IT.
> Abraham Lincoln

USING SYSTEMS TO SUPPORT YOUR FLEXIBLE BUSINESS AND INCREASE PRODUCTIVITY

Creating a flexible, work from anywhere business

Consultants need better ways to monitor customer feedback, sales activity, cash flow, and people issues. As a consultant it is useful to understand the systems that are there to help you and your clients.

I have listed some of the key packages that can support you from Day 1 to allow you to scale quickly and involve other remote working members of your team so that they have access to vital information. There is always a range of admin rights to suit permission levels.

I use all the systems here so am confident to recommend them. I have tried many systems over the years, and they evolve and get better all the time. You may have found alternatives that have been recommended to you too.

Accounting

There are many packages on the marketplace in the UK and other regions of the world aimed at consultants and SMEs.

In my experience some of the most used finance software packages are all cloud based. More details can be found in our book download information. Finances take time if you do not have a cloud system. Now that many tax authorities are needing real time information it has forced people to invest, but this is a great investment to free up your time to focus on your core business and the added value that you bring.

These programmes and apps can be integrated with your business bank account to generate and send invoices and track payments made and received. Data is always available, on any device, allowing for instant decision making.

The other key advantage is your accountant can have a login and support you – advising on VAT, PAYE, and other financial matters. It makes finance for the non-finance manager easy.

Most cloud software is supported with training and live chats so there is plenty of help if you get stuck.

Marketing

There are so many free and good value sites and apps available, and you will find ones that work well for you. Here I highlight a few that I use consistently.

Creating professional marketing materials for social media

Canva
Canva is a tool for design and publishing. It is user-friendly and has thousands of customisable templates. There is a free version which has plenty of options to start with.

Email marketing and database

Mailchimp
The most used software system for email marketing is Mailchimp and there is a free version, with limitations on the size of contacts and campaigns, but it's fine for start-ups.

As their website says, you can "bring your audience data, marketing channels, and insights together so you can reach your goals faster […] you can promote your business across email, social, landing pages, shoppable landing pages, postcards, and more — all from a single platform."

Client relationship management

Capsule CRM

Capsule is a cloud-based Client Relationship Management System – and before you say you are not big enough to have this, trust me you need it!

As you grow your potential clients and suppliers you are going to have hundreds of interactions, many that need follow-up. If you don't have a way of managing this you will forget, overlook, or lose important opportunities.

With Capsule you can keep all your communication with your clients and any files you have sent them easily searchable. If you have other people in the team you add them as a user, and they can then access this too. You can easily allocate follow-up actions to other members of your team and see on a shared dashboard what is happening across the team.

You can add your proposals, so you have visibility of your pipeline and conversion rates. (It's handy to know what works.)

Capsule CRM integrates with many other applications so you don't waste time replicating information across the platforms.

What is HR software?

Human resources (HR) software streamlines all necessary HR functions for human capital management (HCM). Also known as Human Resources Management Systems (HRMS) or Human Resources Information Systems (HRIS), HR software provides a powerful solution for everyday HR processes and strategic planning.

At Breathe, they've developed comprehensive HR software for SMEs. Their award-winning tools put you, as the HR consultant, in control of all HR activities while putting their people at the heart of your clients businesses. It's the perfect solution for keeping on top of your day-to-day HR tasks, centralising data, and maximising employee engagement. As a remote HR service this is ideal for you.

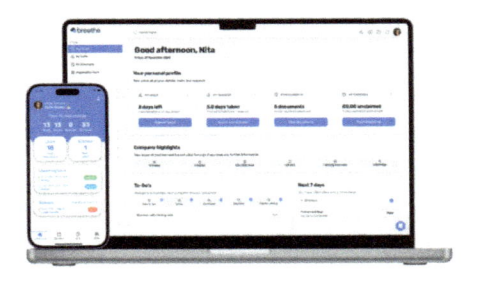

The impact of using cloud technology on your business cannot be underestimated. I have my team based in Athens, Corfu, and the UK and we can all run the business using these systems. You will have the competitive edge over others that choose not to have these systems and you can scale your business easily with the foundations in place from Day 1!

Breathe run a partner programme for consultants. See more details at https://leap-into-consulting.mykajabi.com/Book-Downloads.

If you are a partner, then you get a portal with a demo site on it. If you have staff or associates this is a great way of connecting and demonstrating that you live what you teach!

Other great systems I use

Calendar management
This accelerates people being able to book into your diary without going backwards and forwards checking availability. When I added the link to emails I sent to my clients the uptake on meetings was 80%.

If you are running events or looking to book follow-up calls from webinars this works well. Rest assured it's not a free for all; you can set a number of questions to vet those that want to talk with you and so when the invite drops into your diary you will have prequalified information about them.

A free version is available if you have only one type of meeting – maybe use it for your 20-minute discovery call?

Images for marketing
There are lots of available sites for free images which you can use royalty free. See resources at the end of the book.

Microsoft 365
Microsoft Office 365 is the most common package used for creating documents and managing your emails, calendars, and other productivity features. This of course will be upgraded over time as new features evolve so the name of this may change. Check what functionality you really need and make sure you aren't paying for a package that you won't be using in full.

Solutions for your domain registration, website, and emails

There are many companies offering domain registration for you to register your new business. The company you buy the domain name from doesn't have to be where you host your website or keep your emails. A few of the most common and reliable providers I have used are highlighted in resources at the end of the book.

Whichever provider you choose you are looking for reliability of service and the range of services that they offer you. Most have integrated packages so that you can:

- Register your domain name.
- Build your website and have it hosted.
- Access your emails.

Website building options

Again, there are many companies able to do this for you, in addition to the two I have just mentioned. My two websites are hosted with different companies and both are user-friendly for non-techie people.

To start with you don't need to commission a marketing company to write your website for you or set it up.

Focus on your LinkedIn profile first then set up your website. It is very possible to create your own website with the user friendly options available and the use of AI to support you generating your content.

AUTOMATE TO ELEVATE: HOW HR CONSULTANTS CAN DITCH THE REPETITIVE TASKS AND SCALE WITH EASE

Let's be real—when you became an HR consultant, you probably didn't dream of spending your days chasing invoices, manually scheduling calls, or inputting the same data into multiple systems. Yet here you are, drowning in admin, wondering why you're working harder after leaving the corporate world.

The good news? Automation can rescue you.
By leveraging automation, you can reduce manual tasks, improve efficiency, and free up time to focus on what you actually enjoy—whether that's winning new clients, delivering strategic HR solutions, or sipping a coffee without worrying about your inbox exploding.

Why Automation Matters for HR Consultants
HR consulting isn't just about people—it's also about processes. And let's face it, many of those processes are painfully repetitive. Automating them means:

- **More time for revenue-generating work** – Less admin = more billable hours.
- **Consistent client experience** – No more "Oops, I forgot to send that follow-up email."
- **Faster scaling** – You can grow without burning out or hiring a massive team.
- **Fewer human errors** – Because let's be honest, typos and missed deadlines happen.
- **More work-life balance** – Because working late every night is so corporate.

The Essential Systems to Automate Your HR Consultancy
There's no one-size-fits-all approach, but here are the key types of automation tools every HR consultant should consider:

1. **Client Relationship Management (CRM) Systems** – Keep track of prospects, clients, and every interaction in one place.
   Best for: Managing leads, client onboarding, and follow-ups.

2. **Scheduling & Booking Tools** – No more endless email chains to find a meeting slot.
   Best for: Automating consultations, follow-ups, and calendar invites.

3. **Email & Marketing Automation** – Because sending the same email 50 times is soul-destroying.
   Best for: Email sequences, client updates, newsletters.

4. **Proposal & Contract Automation** – Send professional proposals and contracts in minutes.
   Best for: Streamlining new client sign-ups.

5. **HR & Compliance Systems** – The backbone of your consultancy, ensuring clients stay on track.
   Best for: Managing HR policies, compliance documents, and employee records.

6. **Finance & Invoicing Automation** – Because chasing payments isn't fun.
   Best for: Sending invoices, tracking payments, managing expenses.

7. **Project & Task Management** – Keep everything organised without post-it note chaos.
   Best for: Managing client projects, tracking deliverables.

8. **AI-Powered Chatbots & Virtual Assistants** – Your 24/7 support system.
   Best for: Answering FAQs, client support, lead nurturing.

But What If Your Systems Don't Talk to Each Other?
One of the biggest concerns HR consultants have when setting up automation is dealing with multiple systems that don't integrate. After all, what's the point of automation if you still have to copy and paste data from one tool to another?

Enter Zapier—your secret weapon for connecting all your tools without needing a degree in coding. Zapier acts as the glue between different platforms, allowing them to "talk" to each other and automatically transfer data.

- **New client fills out a form?** Zapier can send their details to your CRM, add them to your email list, and create a new task in your project management tool.
- **Invoice gets paid?** Zapier can update your accounting software, send a thank-you email, and notify you via Slack or email.
- **Someone books a call?** Zapier can add the appointment to your calendar, send a reminder email, and create a follow-up task in your CRM.

With thousands of integrations, Zapier ensures your systems work together, so you don't have to waste time on manual tasks. Think of it as your personal automation assistant—without the payroll costs.

Final Thought: Automate Smarter, Not Harder
Automation isn't about replacing you—it's about making your consultancy work more efficiently so you can focus on growth, strategy, and delivering high-value HR solutions. The right systems will make you look professional, keep clients happy, and—most importantly—give you more time to enjoy the flexibility you built your business for in the first place.

So, if you're still manually sending invoices, chasing emails, and drowning in admin, it's time for a change. Work smarter, not harder—let automation do the heavy lifting.

WELLBEING AND LOOKING AFTER YOURSELF

We have looked at creating systems to improve productivity but what about you? How do you maintain a high level of energy and health?

To start with, you are the business and your health and wellbeing is essential. You have heard my story. The only two occasions I have had business failure have been linked to my health failing. The correlation is that strong. It doesn't have to be that dramatic; it can be low levels of energy, high levels of stress, not exercising or eating properly. They are all linked together.

In this section I share essential healthy tips for you based on many years of self-study in the field of health and wellbeing. For seven years I trained in Amatsu therapy, a complementary therapy looking at all aspects of your health. It originated in Japan and then became westernised to meet the standards necessary to practise in Europe.

Happy and healthy habits

A habit is something you do regularly, without thought, and is usually hard to give up. As a busy consultant it is easy to fall into the trap of putting your life on hold whilst you grow your business and service your clients.

After all, when you are busy how easy is it to take an hour out to go for lunch or a walk when you are under pressure to deliver a project?

I have often put time in my diary for healthy habits like exercise, lunch breaks and generally taking time out. And it's usually the first thing to be replaced when I need extra time.

The consequences are my health – a lack of exercise and stress levels that don't have the time to normalise. Not to mention the impact on your family.

> *"Successful people aren't born that way. They become successful by establishing the habit of doing things unsuccessful people don't like to do."*
>
> *William Makepeace Thackeray*

Movement

You don't have to go for a run but you do need to move your body. Getting a Fitbit or other similar smart device can help you keep track of whether you meet the daily goal of 10,000 steps recommended by many health organisations.

This guidance is taken from the NHS based in the UK and will be updated as research is updated.

> Adults should do some type of physical activity every day. Any type of activity is good for you. The more you do the better. Adults should:
>
> - aim to be physically active every day. Any activity is better than none, and more is better still
> - do strengthening activities that work all the major muscles (legs, hips, back, abdomen, chest, shoulders, and arms) on at least 2 days a week
> - do at least 150 minutes of moderate intensity activity a week or 75 minutes of vigorous intensity activity a week
> - reduce time spent sitting or lying down and break up long periods of not moving with some activity.

If you work in an office or spend most of your day sitting down indoors this can sound difficult to achieve.

The quickest way I managed to hit 10,000 steps a day was when I commuted to London Docklands to see clients and got over 15,000 steps a day, even sitting down for most of the day.

How to hit your 10,000 steps

If you can get out for a walk that is great. If you work from home, why not invest in a mini trampette for your office? I have one of these and I create new ways of getting my 10,000 steps in if the weather isn't so good.

Walking – indoors and outdoors

Every time I am waiting for printing, I get on the trampette and jog – even if it's for a few minutes. I set my alarm for 45-minute chunks so that every 15 minutes in the hour I get up, move, check my emails and generally do non-focused activities.

Walking with a dog is an option many of my clients have.

Standing desks are typically expensive but the principle can be used for Zoom calls – stand when you are in these meetings. If you don't move around too much or get out of breath you can also walk on the spot.

Walk when you are on the mobile – get a pair of Bluetooth headphones to give you the flexibility to move about when you are speaking on the phone (the same tips apply as above!).

Park further away from shops – it's interesting how many steps you can do when you are distracted! A good walk around your high street or shopping centre can clock up the steps easily.

Eating for optimum health

Energy is critical for you to perform at your best.

Barbara Cox is an award-winning nutritionist and businesswoman. She travels across the globe inspiring people to take responsibility for their health and wellness and specialising in corporate wellness strategy and implementation.

Barbara is the author of *Rainbow Recipes* and *Eat to Be Fit* cookbooks and co-author of *The Motorsport Fitness Manual, Teach Yourself Aromatherapy* and *Kitchen Table Tycoon*. She also writes for all major national publications on health and wellness.

Barbara is a guest speaker at some of our events and shares the wealth of her experience with our delegates. She is inspirational to talk to and certainly has bags of energy!

The focus on eating for optimum nutrition is based on a variety of foods that provide you with the necessary nutrients and ensure you have the energy to maintain your health both physically and mentally. The higher the percentage of fresh foods in the diet the better, including an abundance of fruit and vegetables – the full rainbow, which is the underpinning philosophy that many people support, including Barbara.

The lower the percentage of processed foods the better.

I can't do Barbara justice by adding in a few sentences in the book – so it's better to get up-to-date information from her website.

To find out more follow the link https://www.barbaracox.me/

Why is this so important for me to share with you?
I have had decades of intolerances to food and the associated inflammation and low energy that goes with this. After careful deduction I now know

what types of food I need to eat to be healthy and to be able to get out of bed in the morning.

As a consultant it's very easy to slip into bad habits: client lunches, after-work drinks, not eating regularly and eating convenient food on the run.

I used to drive and spend hours in the car, often stopping regularly at motorway services and popping in for a latte (and an extra!). I wondered why in a year I had put so much weight on and was shocked to realise that this one coffee and snack was the equivalent to my whole daily calorie allowance.

Small habits can stop these things happening to you – I'm sure you are more disciplined than I was but I learnt the hard way that a boot full of water, a bag full of apples and some coffee in a flask could save me needing to buy anything and I pay for fuel at the pump now as well.

Without energy you will find it hard to maintain your business focus and success, especially if you are busy.

> *"If your habit doesn't line up with your dream, then you need to either change your habits or change your dream."*
> John Maxwell

Sleep

You may have a Fitbit that monitors your sleep patterns, or you are just aware of how much good quality sleep you get. With levels of uncertainty this can lead to anxiety and worry, two states that can hamper a good night's sleep.

You are likely to experience times as a consultant when you have tight deadlines to deliver, especially when you have many clients. Often cutting back on sleep is an option considered as a way of achieving more.

I have often heard in toxic cultures that sleep is for "pussies" or that Margaret Thatcher only needed four hours a night and that didn't harm her.

Minimum sleep can impact on energy, mood, and ability to concentrate and handle stress.

Over a longer period, this can lead to burnout and then the ability to run a business successfully will be diminished. One of the key reasons why I suggest a business model of having multiple incomes is so important is that it takes the time pressure off you generating income based on your time alone.

> *"The secret to permanently breaking any bad habits is to love something greater than the habit."*
>
> Bryant McGill

TEAM SUPPORT

Having a great team around you will help you grow and focus on what you do best and bring your dream alive.

My team all are self-employed experts in their area. This allows me the flexibility to work with them when the business needs are there, and they have expertise that is very specific.

To be efficient you may need these people in your team, as we have explored already in this chapter. The team you need will depend on where you are with your journey and your availability to invest. Most services can be found easily and as an HR expert you will know how to attract and recruit them. My number one support is my Client Success Manager and my VA. This frees up my time and provides continuity in the business for me and my clients.

Most of the following are nice to haves, depending on your growth plans:

- IT support
- Facebook Adverts and management
- Copywriting
- Online training platforms

There are many websites for tapping into the freelance community worldwide and having specific tasks delegated.

MY GOALS AND ACCOUNTABILITY

Goals are dreams with a deadline

To create outcomes, you need motivation and action. The 90 Day Action Plan aims to kick-start you into focusing on what is important to you in the next three months. It is focused around the "From Corporate to Consulting" Model that you have worked through in Part 2. It is sequential.

You need Confidence and Clarity before you can build your Credibility online and off. Collaborations accelerate your business growth and depth and your Courage will ultimately be what makes you push through on the days you don't feel like it.

90 Day Action Plan

Being focused on what is important will help you drive your success as a consultant.

You can download an editable version of our 90 Day Plan below and from https://leap-into-consulting.mykajabi.com/products/book-downloads.

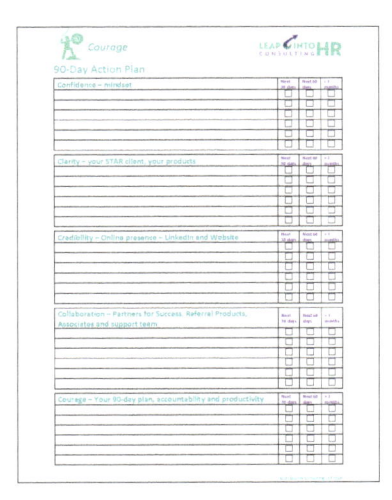

"Motivation is what gets you started. Habit is what keep you going."

Jim Ryun

Your accountability coach

Studies by the American Society of Training and Development show that by having a specific accountability appointment with a person you've committed to, you will increase your chances of success by up to 95%.

You want coaching by someone who has achieved what you want to achieve. All too often I see overinflated guarantees and promises that are great marketing tactics.

Ask to see real results. I offer potential clients the opportunity to talk to my clients and hear for themselves how I work and the results we get together.

Recently I was considering working with a US coaching company and I was concerned about the hype on their website – it all sounded too good to be true. I was keen on their services, but I had a red flag – it was a large investment. I went through the supplier's feedback and recommendations on their site and looked them up on LinkedIn to verify them.

I found someone based in my county and connected with her on LinkedIn and sent a message to her. The supplier agreed to set up a call with her for me to discuss the services and her results. I was beginning to feel more reassured.

The call was very useful and confirmed that the US company were genuine and very good. She even shared some of the reasons why she hadn't done as well, making it clear it was her fault, not the supplier's.

Can you see how even the most impulsive and open-minded people still need to be convinced that the services are right for them?

As a coach I too find it useful to have accountability coaches in my life. And not just one; I look to experts to help accelerate my journey, each with their own specific expertise.

As you start your consulting journey, working with us will give you what you need to get up and running and the confidence to take action. Over time you will specialise and may need expertise in areas that are outside our scope. I do have large networks of coaches and experts to draw from though.

Team accountability community

We have a community for all our bootcamp graduates, called The HR Consultancy Academy® and in it the peer group can help motivate you and reassure you that there is light at the end of the tunnel. It's a group of people on similar journeys, facing similar challenges and with shared experiences.

It's where the magic happens and businesses and people grow.

www.thehrconsultancyacademy.com

YOUR WEEKLY CHECK-INS

You may not have a coach or mentor, but you can still have a business check-in to review your weekly progress. On our bootcamp we have weekly coaching calls and this is a great opportunity to check in on each other as well.

Here are some self-reflection questions:

1. What have I achieved this week?
2. Where am I seeing the results I want?
3. What do I need to stop and review?
4. What negative beliefs have been creeping in this week that have held me back?
5. How many new potential clients have I spoken to?
6. What sales have I achieved?
7. Have I reached out to referral partners this week?
8. What % of my time have I spent on non-billable activities?
9. How have I given back to others in my community this week?
10. Have I maintained a balance of work and personal health?

I am learning a lot about authenticity in business and the expert in this field that I resonate with is George Kao. He has a set of authentic goals and success that he suggests – so I offer these to you as an alternative as well.

Authentic goals and success

1. Am I checking in on a regular basis to audit my activities – which is making the biggest impact on my clients?
2. Which activities can I stop so that I can spend more time with my clients?
3. Have I audited my content in the last month, and what got the most engagement?

4. How can I plan to do more content like this?
5. Every week/day – am I operating my business on my values?
6. Do I need processes to make it sustainable?
7. Can I give back my profits to my affiliates?
8. Can I find simpler way of doing things to make it automated and easier?

These check-ins are a starting point and over time you will create your own versions of this to suit your needs and business.

Working Smarter not Harder

Reflection

Action points

PART 3:
Preparing to Leave the Corporate World

"SOMETIMES THE ONE THING YOU NEED FOR GROWTH IS THE ONE THING YOU ARE AFRAID TO DO."

— SHANNON L. ALDER

Chapter 14:
When is a good time for you?

There will be a range of **life events** that may trigger your need for more flexibility and freedom that may lead to your leap into HR consulting:

- It may be *caring for dependants* including elderly parents and others.

   I also have several women on our bootcamps that are expecting children or returning from maternity leave looking for more flexibility.

- Your own *health needs*. Many people have health conditions which mean that flexibility is needed to maximise their ability to work well. The corporate world typically doesn't afford this flexibility or understanding.

   As I mentioned earlier in the book, I was diagnosed with a chronic condition in 2013, just as I was working in a senior role for an international business. I hadn't realised how much I had relied on flexibility to manage my health, until I found myself in a corporate environment with limited flexibility and high demands for long hours. My health declined quite rapidly and ultimately, I left and became an independent consultant again. Guess what? It improved.

- Your need for a *mobile business*. Maybe you want to have flexibility to move whenever you need to. Maybe your partner is in the military or you would like to travel.

There are also work events that may make you question your need for change:

- Redundancy or risk of redundancy
- The glass ceiling (yes it does still exist)
- A toxic culture
- Being overlooked for promotion

Some people would argue there is never a right time to go into consulting; you just have to do it and make it work for you.

> *"Why fit in when you were born to stand out?"*
> *Dr Seuss*

Fitting in with the crowd is the easy option that requires less work and thought, and it is the path that many choose for the sake of an easy life. By merely fitting in you are denying yourself the opportunity to grow as a person and you are limiting your ability to succeed.

WHAT CROSSROADS ARE YOU AT?

Sometimes, it comes from boredom, as in my case. This can occur especially if you are in a transactional role as an HR business partner with high volumes of similar issues to address.

Whilst my time in retail accelerated my experience of handling high volumes of employee relations issues, after a few years of investigating poor performance, absence, disciplinaries, and grievances it left me wondering if there was more to life than this.

I remember going to Bury St Edmunds to investigate a potential theft case. It was a very long journey to the store and the disciplinary went on for hours. So long in fact that I had to cancel an important dinner date. That was the last time I heard from him and it wasn't the only occasion where my work encroached on my personal life.

In my final role before going into consultancy I had become stifled by process and politics and just couldn't understand why it took so long to make decisions. Maybe I was benchmarking it against the speed of decisions at my dad's business? Whatever the reason, it drove me mad.

Why so slow?

Sometimes you reach this crossroad because of redundancy or something outside of your control.

When you reach a crossroads, it can be terrifying and exciting but many people I have come across in my consulting career also procrastinate, get confused and sometimes take up residence under the signpost.

The key is to revisit your dream, the bigger picture. Does your current role serve you still, is the company the right one for you, or are you ready to move on and set up as an independent consultant?

Recognising the signs that it's time to change

Sometimes it takes events for you to realise that you are at a career crossroads.

Life events make many people really reflect on what is important in their life – have you questioned whether you are on the right path?

We have all learnt a lot from life events, not least how fragile life is and how quickly plans can change.

These may be the signs that you are ready for a change:

- Your manager isn't supporting you.
- You don't feel that you are trusted to get on with your job, without interference.
- Maybe you struggle to get out of bed in the morning?
- Do you feel compromised trying to juggle family and work?
- You don't feel rewarded for all the hard work you put into the business.
- You are sidelined at board level.
- You are creative and have lots of ideas that are not listened to.
- The type of work you are doing is no longer stretching you or creating a challenge.
- Maybe your health is deteriorating?

I am sure you will have you own additional reasons to add here too.

You will have already gone through the chapters on Confidence and Clarity and have answers to how your dreams, skills, and experience are aligned.

Job change v career transition

You may decide that a job change is all that is needed at this stage in your career. This may not be as easy to do now but usually has less impact on others.

Making the move to consulting is a more complex process and is a career transition that is likely to impact on all aspects of your life, even if it's a positive step. Many people also make career transitions by choice.

As you are reading this book it may be that you feel that your current work lacks meaning or purpose. One of the key motivators that new consultants have a high need for on the Motivational Maps profile is Searcher. You can read more about this by clicking https://leap-into-consulting.mykajabi.com/Book-Downloads.

65% of consultants have this as one of their top three motivators.

This need for meaningful work is also supported by the passion to make a difference in other people's lives or to make the world a better place by leaving a legacy. Many consultants go on to write books as a way of fulfilling this ambition.

Once you have decided that consulting is for you, what next?

Again, by now you will have the clarity of the type of consulting business you want and now you need a plan to transition you into consulting, as painlessly as possible.

Many of our HR Consulting bootcamp students start off being employed and transition to consulting over a period of months.

HAVING THE BEST OF BOTH WORLDS

The best of both worlds means reducing your hours in your employed role to three days per week so that you can build your business on the other two days. Given the trend towards more flexible working patterns and business uncertainty I am sure this is a good option for many businesses. They retain your talent, reduce the salary bill and the work you used to do could either be trained up for other people to do or maybe be outsourced to you in a reduced capacity or even as a mentor?

You may need to put a business case together for this option outlining all the benefits for your employer. Or even better if they know you well and understand your future plans then you can discuss the option for reducing hours and when this best suits you both.

Ultimately this will retain your talent and the experience you gain working with many other businesses will give you a broader perspective on issues and solutions that you can incorporate into your employer. In theory it's a win-win situation, although not everyone is open minded enough to see the benefits.

Timing is crucial in case your employer is not open to discuss this as an option. Get your ducks lined up first in case they turn the request down. However, with the current working from home emphasis and uncertainty that exists this may be a great solution.

We have a number of success stories of consultants, in Part 4, that share their journeys in a very honest way. All of these consultants have attended my bootcamp. We also have additional success stories in our online content which you can access.

The key when you reach that crossroads is to gain clarity – and if you have got this far in the book you already have your answer.

Let's Leap into HR Consulting® in a planned way!

Action points

If you are still in an employed role, get even more involved in understanding your business. Know exactly what the commercial goals and strategy are.

See how your HR strategy dovetails into this.

What works? What doesn't work?

What are the barriers for HR in implementing change?

What can you learn from this for when you move into consulting? It's important because these issues won't disappear, but they will impact on how well you implement the project that you have been commissioned to deliver.

Chapter 15:
The change curve

Change Curve

```
                    Focus on
                external environment
                        ↑
Stage 1:                │              Stage 4:
Denial                  │              Commitment

Past  ←─────────────────┼─────────────────→  Future

Stage 2:                │              Stage 3:
Resistance              │              Exploration
                        ↓
                   Focus on self
```

During your transition you may go through highs and lows and I want to share with you how these fit with the change curve.

The change curve is widely used in business and change management, and there are many variations and adaptations. It's often attributed to psychiatrist Elisabeth Kübler-Ross[6], resulting from her work on personal transition in grief and bereavement.

The change curve is a great model that helps you understand the stages you are likely to go through as part of your significant change of direction or career transition.

There are four stages identified in the model that people go through before they adapt to the change fully.

The time in each of these phases will vary depending on the personal circumstances.

Stage 1 – Denial

An event may have triggered your change in direction. It may be redundancy, furloughing, a life event, or some other significant situation. At this stage you may be in denial that these changes are going to take place and maybe you are going along as if nothing is going to happen.

Your morale is likely to be quite high at this stage because as yet it's not really sunk in.

To move from Denial to Resistance you often need to hear the stark truth or see it in black and white.

In your current situation, are you at this stage or further along the curve?

Stage 2 – Resistance

This comes after a realisation that the change is going to take place, and this is usually where all the emotions appear.

If you have chosen the change then you are less likely to have negative emotions – but if you have had change forced on you then you may be angry, frustrated, sad, or bitter. It doesn't really matter what the emotion is; this is part of the natural process of change.

This however is not a place to take up residence, as some people do. You've heard the expression, wallowing in your own self-pity? Well, this is where it is likely to apply.

To move from this stage to the next stage it's about getting a listening ear and support whether it is a coach, mentor, or a friend.

Stage 3 – Exploration

This is where options for moving forward are explored and you need some quick wins to move through this stage before you commit to your new life.

Planning, goal setting and celebrating success are all important here. It is also very easy to slip back into the previous stage if you don't feel you are making progress quickly enough. It's important to celebrate your successes along the journey, no matter how small they are.

I often hear students getting frustrated that they aren't making enough progress and then when I ask them to reflect on what they have achieved in their first three weeks of the bootcamp they have a list that's extremely long. It's about chunking it down into bite-sized pieces, so you see progress.

Stage 4 – Commitment

So, you have your goals and are making your way as a consultant and you think you are committed to the change of career. And then…

Your client doesn't sign the contract, you don't get the engagement from your LinkedIn profile and there is the potential to slip right back to the Resistance stage and reignite emotions of doubt, concern and negativity.

That's why we have a community of like-minded consultants to offer you support and why I am so committed that you have a 90-day plan to keep you on track and not distracted.

> *"Two roads diverged in a wood, and I…*
> *I took the one less travelled by,*
> *and that has made all the difference."*
>
> *Robert Frost*

A MOUNTAIN OF CONCERNS

If you were to do a list of all the concerns you had about going into consulting now, they would probably outweigh the benefits. And this makes sense because at this stage you are unable to predict the other rewards that might not be so obvious.

For example, who would have listed a better relationship with their partner as a benefit of going into consulting?

Taking the Leap into Consulting® is not as irrational as it sounds and driven by impulse as it might appear.

When you have that spark of desire for a better future that hits all your dreams why wouldn't you do it? Well where do I start…

As I have mentioned before, many people I talk to have their dreams crushed by "I'm just going to run it by my partner" to find that they are not so thrilled about the new dream as they are. Often, I see people held back by the lack of support.

For those that are truly able to follow their dream it's described by my clients as the best thing they ever did. It's all about how you frame the move and also being prepared so that the transition doesn't impact on your family and income.

If you wait until you're ready you'll be waiting the rest of your life.

Chapter 16:
Creating an income from Day 1

SO HOW DO YOU CREATE AN INCOME FROM DAY 1?

Time to get those ducks lined up

When I talk to people like you that are about to take the leap, they often say that they have had discussions with the ex-employer/friends/family/friends of family that are keen to work with them. I am unsure why people promise "potential" work so freely. Do they think it's helpful?

Top tip – assume that it won't happen and look for other new business opportunities.

Network like mad for your first three months; go to every networking event where your potential clients hang out. If you are working your notice, then take advantage of this period to start this process now. Start talking about your future, have your business cards to hand and start the dialogue immediately.

As you are an HR professional, you'll also know that this mustn't be done in company time or conflict with where you are currently. The last thing you need is to be dismissed for gross misconduct!

"But I can't do sales"

Today I was delighted to read one of the comments in our HR Consultancy Academy® group from a bootcamper (a person that has completed our six-week HR Consulting Bootcamp programme).

She said that she was enjoying networking and could not believe she said it as the thought of it used to terrify her.

Have you just had that fear run through your head that you can't "do sales" and hate networking?

Yes, you can!

In your current role day in, day out, you are networking with your peers, across the business, with senior managers and a variety of diverse people. You listen to their needs; you work with them to create a solution and then you support them in the delivery of this.

Being able to create an income is essential to survive in a business, but you don't have to "do sales" to get this. This is an outdated thought process. You are skilled at building rapport and influencing others, and these are the key attributes for success along with the clarity of how you can solve your potential clients' problems, unmet needs, or desires.

How would you rate the following skills out of 10?

- Rapport-building ability
- Being able to influence
- Listening attentively

Your aim is to have work signed up before you leave employment. Act now. The sales cycle in consulting takes typically 1–3 months or more and a sale isn't a sale until the money is in your bank account.

QUICK WINS – GETTING YOUR IDEAL CLIENTS

I have mentioned before the importance of clarifying your ideal client (see Chapter 10 – Clarity).

Business to Business (B2B)

When you first go into consulting consider the SME marketplace as a good starting point. It's much quicker to meet decision makers and build long-term relationships when the MD is the owner of the business. They rarely leave!

Focusing on corporates normally means a long procurement process with tenders that you may or may not get feedback on. It's a time consuming and costly business when you are setting up to do these and as a rookie consultant it is very difficult to get these contracts.

Once you have a track history and a few years of accounts, case studies, and testimonials these doors will be easier to open.

Managing directors/owners and HR managers/directors
Your ideal clients are likely to be a combination of MDs/owners of SMEs (up to 250 employees) or HR managers/professionals of larger organisations.

The two target markets are completely different, and they unfortunately rarely share the same room. Their needs are different and engaging with them will need a different focus.

1. Managing directors of SMEs
MDs want to know what you can offer their business, who you have worked with, what results you have achieved and what guarantees you will make. They do not understand or want to hear HR jargon. I cannot stress this enough. They have no interest in what you have done for large corporates. They are smaller businesses with limited resources and a real desire to

grow and create wealth for the shareholders and profits for reinvesting and growth.

Your primary goal is to link HR into their business plans and to relieve them of their people headaches.

If you are not commercially savvy or have little experience of working with SMEs start reading about what is going on for owners and entrepreneurs.

Wherever you are located you will have local business groups targeted to your ideal clients.

And if you want to target businesses near you then you can keep up to date with business news in your local newspaper and local Facebook groups.

It takes time to specialise in a niche area so you will not be expected to be an expert from Day 1 but you will definitely have an advantage if you can speak their language and have experience of contributing at board level.

Working at board level in an SME is very different to a corporate board. The pace of decisions is usually quicker in SMEs and there is usually more agility to make things happen.

2. HR departments

The needs, desires, and wants of an HR manager will be different. They understand the jargon; they are an HR professional. Often consultants are engaged for the following reasons:

- You have expertise that the in-house team don't have.
- The team have the expertise but don't have time, given the deadlines to deliver a project.
- The project or problem needs someone that is external and perceived to be more objective.

If you are an HR business partner currently your skills and approach will transfer easily across to consulting. You are fulfilling a need to work in partnership for your HR client to deliver a project internally. The level of involvement will vary for each client from full involvement and exposure within the business to only delivering work for the commissioning HR client.

Rarely will you be asked to come in as an HR generalist. You will be focused on a very specific project.

So what skills, experience, or knowledge do you have that will make you attractive as a consultant? For example, are you an employee engagement specialist or an executive team build facilitator?

Business to consumer (B2C)

With the growth of coaching and mentoring you may be targeting individuals rather than businesses. This is a different way to market but with social media it is also easier.

Whichever route you go down it's all about relationships, building, and nurturing in an authentic manner. If you don't care for your clients, they will spot it a mile off and your business is likely to end up with a lot of one-off projects. It's hard work to maintain this model commercially.

When you complete the self-review questionnaire as part of our courses you get a clear idea of how your preferences and motivators will impact on how you work with your clients and the type of consulting that will suit you best.

Chapter 17:
You are thinking of resigning now!

TOP TIPS BEFORE YOU RESIGN

The urge to leave, I am sure, is great but unless you have financial stability, I would recommend a planned, slightly slower exit.

1. Look at options for reducing your full-time hours to part time to allow you the stability to dip your toe into the water first.

2. Resign and then support your employer on an ad hoc basis.

3. Pull together examples of projects that you have delivered successfully inhouse and create mini case studies with ROIs.

4. "Act as if": approach your role as if you are already an HR consultant.

5. Have clarity around your future business.

6. Increase your social media presence – change your profiles to reflect outcomes and successes. Have copy ready for the final switchover when you leave.

7. Have a website ready to launch (not essential).

8. Have business cards ready to hand out – remember that quality is important.

9. Decide on a name for your business and logo which reflects what you do and who you are.

10. Create a business bank account and create a business structure after discussion with an accountant.

11. Check out grants and loans for start-ups.

12. Have a one-page flyer for your business (PDF).

13. Network like crazy in the places your future clients will be (out of hours).

14. Join support and coaching groups, online and offline. Build a team around you.

Accelerating your transition into consulting with a structure is core to our HR Consulting Bootcamps, which are designed to launch your business successfully in a six-week period.

Please don't "leave it and see how it goes". I have heard this so many times. You can choose the long hard way to set up your business or you can accelerate your success and enjoy the journey, have some fun and have a community around you for support.

New is always challenging to some degree. Exciting maybe, but also hard especially as you are going from being knowledgeable and an expert in your field to being a newbie as a consultant. You may miss your need to be "an expert" but soon you will learn the ropes and really know what you are doing and enjoy it. It's a learning curve that I am sure you will thrive on, even though it might feel bewildering to start with.

Reflection

Action points

PART 4:
The First 12 Months of Your Business

Consistency is more important than perfectionism.

Chapter 18:
The First Year of Running an HR Consultancy: The Highs, The Lows, and The Must-Do's

THE 'OH WOW, I'VE ACTUALLY DONE IT' MOMENT

So, you've finally taken the leap from corporate HR to running your own consultancy. Congratulations! You're officially the boss, the strategist, the marketer, and, let's be honest, the tea-maker. That initial thrill of setting up your own business is intoxicating—until you realise that being your own boss also means dealing with your tax office, finding clients, and learning how to send an invoice that doesn't look like it was made in Microsoft Paint circa 1998.

Priorities:

- **Get clear on your why** – You left corporate life for a reason. Keep that front and centre.
- **Set up the basics** – Business structure, bank accounts, and legal essentials (yes, you actually do need terms of business!).
- **Find your first clients** – Because 'build it and they will come' is a lovely idea, but reality prefers a solid marketing plan.

The Feast, the Famine, and the Fear Factor

Month three rolls around, and suddenly, you realise client work doesn't just fall from the sky. Welcome to the 'feast or famine' cycle. One minute you're drowning in work, the next you're wondering if you should start an Etsy shop for motivational HR quotes (spoiler: 'Because I said so' doesn't sell as well as you think).

How to Tackle It:
- **Pipeline is everything** – Even when you're busy, keep networking, marketing, and prospecting. Future-you will thank you.
- **Price for profit** – No more 'mate's rates' or 'just getting started' discounts. You're a business, not a charity.
- **Budget like a CFO** – Your income will fluctuate, so plan for it. A business savings cushion is your best friend.

Clients from Heaven (and the Other Place)

Some clients will be an absolute dream—pay on time, value your work, and tell everyone they know about you. Others... well, let's just say you'll learn the art of setting boundaries quickly. The first time a client ghosts you on payment, you'll wish you had stronger terms of business (which, by the way, you need).

Lessons Learned:
- **Contracts matter** – Always have a signed agreement. Handshakes and good intentions don't pay bills.
- **Red flags are real** – If they haggle over price before work starts, expect issues later.
- **Overdeliver within reason** – Give great value, but don't let 'just a quick chat' turn into hours of unpaid consulting.

The Rollercoaster of Confidence

Running a consultancy is a confidence game. One day, you're nailing client pitches and feeling unstoppable. The next, you're convinced you'll be out of business by Friday.

Building Resilience:
- **Celebrate wins** – However small. Landed a new client? Survived a tough negotiation? Treat yourself.
- **Find a support network** – Other HR consultants, mentors, business groups—people who get it.
- **Keep learning** – Whether it's sales, marketing, or AI in HR, staying ahead keeps you competitive. Look into joining our HR Consultancy Academy® for ongoing learning and support.

The First-Year Finish Line

Before you know it, you'll be at the one-year mark. You'll have stories—some triumphant, some cringe-worthy—but most importantly, you'll still be standing. Success in year one isn't about perfection; it's about persistence, adaptability, and knowing that every misstep is just part of the process.

Reflections for Success:
- **Know your numbers** – Revenue, profit, and cash flow should be familiar terms, not mysteries.
- **Revisit your strategy** – What worked? What flopped? Adjust accordingly.
- **Plan for year two** – Because if year one was a learning curve, year two is where you start to thrive.

Running an HR consultancy isn't for the faint-hearted, but with the right mindset, the right strategies, and a little bit of humour, you'll build something truly rewarding. And remember—every successful consultant once had a first year, too. You've got this.

Chapter 19:
How to Find Clients as an HR Consultant
(Without Losing Your Mind)

So, you've taken the leap into HR consulting®. Congratulations! Now comes the small matter of finding clients. If you thought writing policies on conflict resolution was tricky, just wait until you're staring at your laptop, wondering where to find people willing to pay for your expertise.

20 TRIED AND TESTED WAYS TO GET MORE CLIENTS

Fear not! Here are 20 tried-and-tested (and occasionally fun) ways to fill your client roster without resorting to interpretive dance in your local business park.

1. LinkedIn Lurking (With Purpose!)

You're an HR consultant, which means LinkedIn should be your second home. Connect with HR Directors, CEOs, and other decision-makers who fit into your ideal client category. Post valuable content, comment on discussions, and for the love of all things professional, update your profile. If your tagline still says "seeking new opportunities," we need to talk. Please attend one of our LinkedIn webinars to get started !

2. Ex-Colleagues & Corporate Escapees
Remember all those people you used to work with? The ones who said, "If I ever leave, I'd totally hire you"? Time to call in those favours. Drop them a message and remind them you're now in the business of saving them from HR disasters.

3. HR Networking Events (Yes, Even the Awkward Ones)
Love them or hate them, networking events work. But don't just show up, sip lukewarm coffee, and hope for the best. Set a goal (e.g., meet five new people) and have your cards ready and know how to connect with your LinkedIn profile. Combine face to face events along with virtual and consistency is important – become familiar in the groups that you belong to.

4. Webinars & Workshops
Hosting a free (but valuable!) webinar on how to avoid HR nightmares is a great way to showcase your expertise. People love free stuff. Once they hear how brilliant you are, they'll wonder how they ever survived without you. Most people now use this as a way to increase expert positioning as well as an efficient way to connect with multiple people.

5. Speak at Conferences (Or at Least Pretend to Love Public Speaking)
HR conferences are crawling with potential clients. Get on the speaker list and share insights on something juicy like "Why Your Performance Management System is Killing Morale". By the end, someone will be asking for your business card. Start small if this isn't your thing yet and work your way up to the larger events. I now enjoy speaking and have done the CIPD events in London – but when I started out a room of 8 delegates was bad enough for me .

6. Collaborate with Other Consultants

Know someone who offers legal advice, finance support, or business coaching? Team up! Cross-referrals can work wonders, and suddenly, you're introduced to a whole new client base. Be active in our Facebook Group where you can connect and collaborate (details at the end of the book).

7. Facebook Groups & Online Communities

Find entrepreneur groups, business owner forums, and even local small business groups where people ask HR-related questions. Be helpful, offer advice (without sounding salesy), and watch those DMs roll in.

8. Guest on HR & Business Podcasts

No, you don't need to start your own podcast (unless you want to), but being a guest on someone else's? Absolutely. Share your expertise and make sure you have a strong call to action at the end. We have regular guests on our podcast – Leap into HR Consulting® – talking about their journey into consulting and I also am a guest on other podcasts. It's a great way to reach a larger international audience and grow your presence.

9. Write a Killer Blog (That's Not Boring)

If you can write, use it. Share valuable insights on your website or LinkedIn. But please—no jargon-filled HR essays. If it sounds like a legal handbook, people will snooze before they finish the first paragraph. Tap into what the keys issues are that are facing your ideal client. Use your personality and AI and this will help overcome any writers blocks.

10. Case Studies & Testimonials

Got a happy client? Get them to shout about it! Case studies show potential clients what you can do, and glowing testimonials help people trust you faster. Create graphics and also ensure that they are added to our LinkedIn profile under the recommendations section.

11. Run a Challenge (People Love a Good Challenge)
Host a 5-day HR Fix-Up Challenge where business owners can audit their HR practices. Give them a taste of your magic, and soon they'll want more. Make it simple to do and engage with those taking part to add real value.

12. Direct Outreach (Yes, Cold Emails Work—When Done Right)
A well-crafted, non-spammy email to a business owner can open doors. Keep it short, relevant, and focused on how you can solve their pain points. Again, if this isn't your first love get support and use AI to help craft content.

13. Offer a Free HR Checklist or Template
Who doesn't love a freebie? Create something genuinely useful—like an HR Compliance Checklist for Small Businesses—and offer it in exchange for an email. Now you have leads! You don't need a website to do this you could add it as a lead magnet to your social media – especially LinkedIn or maybe Facebook Ads.

14. Partner with Co-Working Spaces
Co-working spaces are filled with businesses that need HR help. Offer to run a free HR Q&A session or leave behind some flyers. This is how I started out – in an incubator hub for new businesses – it was great value – good fun and was lovely to get out of the house.

15. Join Local Business Groups
Chambers of Commerce, networking groups, and business breakfast clubs are great for meeting potential clients. Plus, who doesn't love a cooked breakfast while networking?

Try the groups before you commit and once you have found your tribe turn up on a regular basis – you need to get known in that group – that familiar face! Oh and it's ok if there's already an HR Consultant on the group – there's plenty of space for you too.

16. Social Media Visibility (But Make It Fun)
Instagram and TikTok aren't just for dance challenges. Share HR tips, client success stories, and even a few HR horror stories (anonymously, of course). Engage, entertain, and educate! However, if you are limited for time – focus on LinkedIn.

17. Offer a 'Pick My Brain' Call
Short 20-minute calls where people can ask you one HR question (for free). Many will realise they need more help and hire you. We use these calls in our coaching business and there is real value for your client and for us in exploring the opportunity to work together. Only yesterday a lady on a call said she was amazed at how useful the 20 minutes was.

18. Corporate Memberships & Associations
Join our HR Consulting community, other business communities, and associations where potential clients hang out. Being listed as an expert in these spaces can bring credibility and clients.

19. Referral Incentives (Because People Like Rewards)
Tell your existing clients or contacts that if they refer someone to you, they get a little thank-you gift (or a discount on future services). We offer a referral programme which we love because who better to promote your business than someone who has benefited from your services already.

20. Just Ask!
Seriously. Tell your network, family, and friends that you're looking for clients. You'd be surprised who knows someone who needs HR support.

SKILLS & BEHAVIOURS FOR SUCCESS IN FINDING CLIENTS

Attracting and retaining clients as an HR consultant requires more than just technical HR expertise—it demands a combination of business acumen, interpersonal skills, and strategic thinking. To build a sustainable and successful consultancy, you need to develop the following key skills and behaviours:

1. Confidence & Resilience
Rejection is part of the journey, and persistence is essential. Clients won't always say yes immediately, and overcoming setbacks with confidence is key to long-term success. The ability to keep going despite challenges separates thriving consultants from those who struggle.

2. Strong Communication
Effectively articulating your value to potential clients makes all the difference. Whether it's through emails, discovery calls, or presentations, the way you convey your expertise and solutions can determine whether a lead converts into a client.

3. Networking & Relationship Building
Successful HR consultants don't just find clients; they build long-term relationships. Knowing where to network, how to engage with potential clients, and nurturing relationships for future opportunities is a crucial skill.

4. Problem-Solving Ability
Clients seek HR consultants who provide actionable solutions, not just advice. Understanding their pain points and offering tailored, results-driven strategies will position you as an indispensable partner.

5. Marketing & Personal Branding
Establishing credibility online is non-negotiable in today's world. A strong LinkedIn presence, compelling content, and a clear personal brand help you attract the right clients and position yourself as an expert in your niche.

6. Empathy & Emotional Intelligence

HR is people-centric, and so is consulting. Understanding the emotional and business challenges of your clients builds trust and strengthens relationships, leading to repeat business and referrals.

7. Adaptability & Continuous Learning

The HR landscape is constantly evolving. Staying ahead of trends, legal updates, and best practices ensures you remain relevant and in demand. Continuous professional development is key to maintaining your competitive edge.

8. Negotiation & Sales Skills

Many HR consultants struggle with selling their services. Learning how to confidently price your offerings, negotiate contracts, and close deals effectively is essential to securing consistent income and business growth.

Want to Develop These Skills and Secure More Clients?

If you're serious about building a successful HR consultancy, joining The HR Consultancy Academy® is your next step. Our Academy provides:

- **Training & Resources** – Develop your skills in sales, marketing, and client acquisition.
- **Expert Guidance** – Learn from seasoned HR consultants who have built thriving businesses.
- **Networking & Community** – Connect with like-minded professionals and potential referral partners.
- **Business Growth Support** – Practical strategies to attract, win, and retain clients effectively.
- **HR Consulting Marketplace** - A sophisticated directory to connect you to potential clients.

As you review your skills and behaviours, consider using your DISC profile to better understand your strengths and areas for improvement. Whether you're more dominant, influential, steady, or conscientious, knowing your behavioural style can help you tailor your client approach, improve communication, and enhance your overall consulting effectiveness.

TOOLS & SYSTEMS TO IMPROVE CONVERSION RATES

Converting prospects into paying clients is a crucial aspect of running a successful HR consultancy. The right tools and systems can help streamline this process, ensuring that no lead is overlooked and that your outreach is efficient and professional.

Here are some essential categories of tools that can enhance your client conversion process:

1. CRM Systems
A Customer Relationship Management (CRM) system helps you organise and track leads, manage follow-ups, and automate workflows. By keeping all client interactions in one place, you can ensure no opportunity slips through the cracks and personalise your communication based on client history.

2. Email Marketing & Automation
Consistent and value-driven communication nurtures leads and builds trust. Email marketing platforms allow you to send targeted campaigns, automate follow-ups, and engage prospects with relevant content that moves them closer to making a decision.

3. Scheduling & Booking Software
Streamline the process of booking discovery calls and consultations by using online scheduling tools. These systems eliminate back-and-forth emails by allowing clients to choose a convenient time, reducing friction in the client journey.

4. Proposal & Contract Management
Speed up the onboarding process by using digital proposal and contract tools. These platforms allow you to send professional proposals, secure electronic signatures, and automate contract approvals—ensuring a seamless and efficient client experience.

5. Sales Funnel & Lead Capture Platforms

Guiding potential clients from initial interest to conversion requires a structured approach. Lead capture and sales funnel platforms help automate the process, from landing pages and email sequences to payment and onboarding, ensuring a smooth transition from prospect to client.

6. Social Media Management

Maintaining a strong and consistent online presence is essential for building credibility. Social media management tools allow you to schedule posts, track engagement, and manage multiple platforms efficiently, helping you stay visible to your audience without overwhelming your schedule.

Want to Learn How to Use These Tools Effectively?

Having the right systems in place is only half the battle—knowing how to use them strategically is what truly improves your conversion rates.

The HR Consultancy Academy® provides expert guidance on selecting, setting up, and leveraging these tools to grow your business. Through tailored training, hands-on support, and a community of like-minded consultants, you'll learn how to:

- Automate and optimise your client journey
- Streamline your sales and onboarding processes
- Build and nurture relationships effectively
- Improve efficiency while staying client-focused

REGIONAL DIFFERENCES: UK, USA, CANADA, AUSTRALIA

While the core strategies for attracting and converting clients apply globally, there are important regional nuances to consider. Understanding these differences can help HR consultants tailor their approach and maximise opportunities in each market.

United Kingdom (UK)

The UK has a well-established HR consulting market, with strict employment laws and a strong emphasis on compliance. Many SMEs seek external HR support to navigate regulations, making expertise in employment law and employee relations highly valued.

- CIPD qualifications and other accreditations can enhance credibility, as many businesses prefer working with HR professionals who hold recognised qualifications. However, in my experience, most business owners will just want to know you can help them and won't be hung up on this.
- Networking groups for SMEs and HR professionals provide excellent opportunities to connect with potential clients. Many small business owners seek HR support at local business events.
- A strong understanding of UK employment law and tribunal processes is essential, as businesses often require guidance on redundancy, disciplinaries, and workplace disputes.

United States (USA)

HR outsourcing is common in the USA due to the complexity of federal and state employment laws. Many businesses prefer to work with HR consultants to ensure compliance across different states.

- State-specific HR expertise is crucial, as employment laws vary widely. Demonstrating knowledge of regional compliance can set you apart.

- SHRM (Society for Human Resource Management) events and networking groups offer access to business owners looking for HR support.
- Chambers of Commerce and small business networks provide valuable opportunities to connect with companies that do not have in-house HR teams.
- Employee benefits and healthcare management are key areas where businesses seek HR consultancy due to the complexity of health insurance and workplace benefits regulations.

Canada

Canada's HR landscape is heavily influenced by employment law, and HR consultants frequently collaborate with employment lawyers to provide businesses with well-rounded advice.

- HRPA (Human Resources Professionals Association) membership is beneficial, as it is one of the leading professional bodies in Canada.
- Employment law expertise is in high demand, particularly around contracts, workplace investigations, and terminations.
- Local business associations and networking groups are great places to find smaller businesses that need HR guidance, particularly in compliance-heavy industries.
- French-English bilingualism can be an asset, especially for HR consultants working in Quebec, where language laws impact HR policies and documentation.

Australia

The Australian market presents strong opportunities for HR consultants, particularly in supporting small businesses that do not have in-house HR teams.

- Small & medium sized businesses are the primary clients for HR consultants, as many do not have dedicated HR departments.
- LinkedIn networking is highly effective, with many business owners seeking HR support through online connections.

- Co-working hubs and business incubators are excellent places to find start-ups and growing businesses in need of HR guidance.
- AHRI (Australian HR Institute) events and memberships provide credibility and access to a network of HR professionals and potential clients.
- Workplace health and safety regulations are a key area where businesses often require external HR expertise, particularly in industries such as construction and healthcare.

Tailoring Your Approach for Maximum Impact

By understanding the unique challenges and opportunities in each region, HR consultants can better position their services and connect with the right clients. Whether it's leveraging professional memberships, networking strategically, or specialising in region-specific employment laws, adapting to local market needs is key to success.

Now, pick three strategies from this list and take action today. Your dream clients are out there—they just need to find you first!

THE BUSINESS DEVELOPMENT CYCLE FOR HR CONSULTANTS: A STEP-BY-STEP GUIDE

Setting up and growing an HR consultancy requires Clarity on your niche, Confidence in your expertise, Credibility to attract clients, Collaboration with key partners, and Courage to scale and innovate. Below is a structured approach aligned with the $^{5C's}$ Model of Corporate to Consulting to help you navigate the journey from launch to long-term success.

1. Market Research & Positioning (Defining Your Niche)

Clarity is essential before launching your HR consultancy. You must define who you help and how you help them. You have touched on this in our chapters on Clarity & Credibility.

Key Steps:
- **Identify Your Niche** – Focus on industries or business sizes you best serve, such as:
    - Small & medium sized businesses
    - Start-ups
    - Healthcare organisations
    - Professional services firms (law, accountancy, IT)
    - Manufacturing and engineering businesses
- **Define Your Ideal Client Profile (ICP)** – Consider:
    - Number of employees
    - Common HR challenges (e.g. compliance, recruitment, leadership training)
    - Budget for HR consulting services
- **Research Competitors** – Understand their offerings, pricing, and differentiators.
- **Create Your Unique Value Proposition (UVP)** – Clearly state how your services solve problems better than competitors.

- Example: "Helping businesses build HR processes that reduce staff turnover by 30% in the first year."
- **Develop Your Brand Identity** – A professional brand boosts Credibility:
    - A website showcasing services, testimonials, and case studies.
    - A strong LinkedIn presence.
    - Consistent branding across all platforms.

2. Lead Generation & Marketing (Attracting Potential Clients)

Once you have Clarity on your audience, focus on building Confidence in your services and establishing Credibility.

Key Strategies:
- **Networking & Relationship Building** (Courage & Collaboration)
    - Attend HR and business networking events (e.g. CIPD & SHRM conferences, business forums).
    - Join LinkedIn groups and forums where your target clients are active.
- **Content Marketing** (Confidence & Credibility)
    - Publish LinkedIn articles, blogs, or host webinars/podcasts on HR challenges.
    - Share case studies to highlight success stories.
- **Referral Partnerships** (Collaboration)
    - Partner with accountants, employment lawyers, or business coaches who can refer clients.
    - Offer incentives for referrals (e.g. a free consultation for every new client referral).
- **Email Campaigns & Paid Ads**
    - Build an email list of business owners needing HR support.
    - Run LinkedIn or Google ads targeting your niche.

3. Sales & Client Acquisition (Turning Interest into Paying Clients)

Transforming leads into paying clients requires Confidence in your sales approach and a clear Credibility-building process.

Key Steps:
1. **Discovery Call** – A free consultation to assess client needs.
2. **Offer a Free Resource** – An HR audit checklist or short training session to build trust.
3. **Proposal & Pricing** – Clearly outline services, deliverables, and pricing models.
    - Retainer (monthly fee for ongoing support)
    - Project-Based (specific deliverables)
    - Hourly Rate (advice or coaching)
4. **Contract Agreement** – Protects both you and the client.
5. **Onboarding New Clients** – Set expectations with a welcome email, project timeline, and first steps.

4. Service Delivery & Client Engagement (Delivering Value to Clients)

Delivering exceptional HR solutions strengthens Credibility and builds lasting relationships.

Key Strategies:
- **Clear Communication** – Keep clients updated via emails, meetings, and progress reports.
- **Deliver Measurable Results** – Show tangible impacts like reduced turnover or improved compliance.
- **Use Client Feedback** – Regularly ask for feedback to refine your services.

5. Retention & Upselling
(Building Long-Term Client Relationships)

Building strong client relationships requires Collaboration and the Courage to expand your offerings.

Key Strategies:
- **Offer Ongoing HR Support** – Transition project-based clients into long-term advisory retainers.
- **Introduce New Services** – Adapt as clients grow (e.g. HR strategy planning, executive coaching).
- **Stay in Touch** – Engage past clients with newsletters and follow-ups.
- **Ask for Referrals** – Happy clients will refer others if you ask.

6. Scaling & Growth
(Expanding Your HR Consulting Business)

Scaling your business requires Courage to take calculated risks and Collaboration to build a supportive network.

Key Growth Strategies:
- **Automate or Delegate** – Use virtual assistants or automation tools for admin tasks.
- **Expand Your Services** – Introduce diversity & inclusion programs or mental health support.
- **Collaborate with Other Consultants** – Partner with specialists to increase value.
- **Increase Prices Strategically** – Adjust fees as your experience and reputation grow.
- **Create Passive Income Streams** – Offer online courses, templates, or membership programmes.

Final Thoughts

The Business Development Cycle for HR consultants requires **Confidence** in your skills, **Clarity** in your strategy, **Credibility** to attract clients, **Collaboration** for referrals and partnerships, and **Courage** to scale and innovate. By applying these principles, you can create a thriving, sustainable HR consultancy that continues to evolve and succeed.

The Business Development Cycle for HR Consultants: A Step-by-Step Approach

Journey to Success: Creating Your Roadmap

Introduction

Success is not a destination but a journey. This worksheet will help you design a roadmap to achieve your personal and professional goals. By defining your vision, setting clear objectives, and taking strategic action, you can create a path to success that is achievable and sustainable.

Step 1: Define Your Vision

Exercise: Write down your vision for success.

- Where do you see yourself in 1, 3, or 5 years?
- What impact do you want to make?
- What excites and motivates you about this journey?

Your Vision Statement:

_____
_____
_____
_____
_____
_____

Step 2: Set SMART Goals

SMART Goals Framework:

- Specific – Clearly define what you want to achieve.
- Measurable – Set criteria for tracking progress.
- Achievable – Ensure it is realistic given your resources.
- Relevant – Align it with your long-term vision.
- Time-bound – Set a deadline for completion.

Exercise: Write down 3 SMART goals for your journey to success.

1. _____

2. _____

3. _____

Step 3: Assess Your Starting Point

SWOT Analysis: Identify your strengths, weaknesses, opportunities, and threats.

Strengths   Weaknesses

Opportunities   Threats

Reflection: What are the key areas you need to work on?

_____
_____
_____
_____

Step 4: Break It Down into Milestones

Milestone Planning:

- Short-term (30-90 days): Quick wins to build momentum.
- Medium-term (6-12 months): Achievements that bring you closer to success.
- Long-term (1-3 years): The bigger vision taking shape.

Exercise: Write down your key milestones.

Short-term: _____

Medium-term: _____

Long-term: _____

Step 5: Identify Key Actions & Resources

List the actions you need to take to achieve each milestone.

Milestone	Key Actions	Resources Needed

Step 6: Build Accountability & Track Progress

Accountability Strategies:

- Set up weekly/monthly check-ins.
- Use tracking tools (Google Sheets, Trello, Notion).
- Find an accountability partner or mentor.
- Celebrate small wins.

Exercise:

Who will hold you accountable? _____

_____

_____

How will you track progress? _____

_____

_____

How will you reward yourself for small achievements?

_____

_____

_____

Step 7: Adapt & Evolve

Success requires flexibility. Be prepared to pivot, learn from failures, and adjust your strategy.

Reflection:

What challenges do you anticipate? How will you overcome them?
_____
_____
_____
_____

How will you stay motivated through setbacks?
_____
_____
_____
_____

Final Action Plan

Summarise your roadmap in a simple action plan.

Goal	Milestones	Key Actions	Deadline

PART 5 || YOUR FIRST 12 MONTHS

Final Thoughts

Success is a continuous journey. By following this roadmap, you will have a clear direction, take intentional actions, and stay committed to your goals. Review your progress regularly and adjust your plan as needed.

You have the power to create your success—now go and make it happen!

You can download a version of this worksheet from our resources page.

You can't change the wind but you can tack to adjust your course…

YOUR NEXT STEPS

The HR Consultancy Academy®: Supporting HR Consultants in Your Professional Journey

Why The HR Consultancy Academy® Exists

The HR Consultancy Academy® was created to provide a structured, supportive, and high-value learning environment for HR professionals transitioning into or growing their consulting businesses. Recognising the unique challenges HR consultants face—such as navigating self-employment, developing a commercial mindset, and maintaining professional growth—The HR Consultancy Academy® bridges the gap between traditional HR roles and successful consultancy practices.

Our mission is to equip HR consultants with the knowledge, confidence, and community they need to thrive in an increasingly competitive market. Many HR professionals have the technical expertise but struggle with the business acumen required to attract clients, price their services effectively, and scale their offerings. The HR Consultancy Academy® was built to solve these challenges, ensuring that HR consultants don't have to figure it all out alone.

What The HR Consultancy Academy® Provides

The Academy is more than just a learning platform—it is an active and engaged community of HR professionals dedicated to mutual success. Here's what members gain:

- **Exclusive Training & Resources** – Access to expert-led webinars, toolkits, and guides designed specifically for HR consultants, covering topics such as business development, pricing strategies, marketing, legal considerations, and consulting frameworks.

- **Live Expert Q&A Sessions** – Monthly co-branded live sessions with industry experts providing deep insights into HR consulting, finance, automation, marketing, and legal aspects. Members have the opportunity to ask questions and gain real-time advice.

- **Personalised Growth Roadmap** – Each member receives a customised roadmap to help them define their goals, develop their services, and scale their consulting business in a structured way.

- **Networking & Community** – A dedicated community of like-minded HR consultants for peer support, referrals, and knowledge-sharing. This includes an exclusive online group where members can connect, collaborate, and support one another.

- **Quarterly Sprint Planning** – A structured approach to goal setting, ensuring members stay focused on their next 90-day business objectives with clear strategies and accountability.

- **Exclusive Discounts & Perks** – Members benefit from exclusive deals, such as a discount on CIPD HR Inform, FSB membership, and other valuable offers that enhance their consulting practice.

- **Ongoing Professional Development** – The HR Consultancy Academy® ensures HR consultants stay ahead of industry trends, client expectations, and emerging business opportunities, allowing them to continuously enhance their skills and service offerings.

The Annual HR Consultancy Academy Festival

A key highlight of The HR Consultancy Academy® is the annual HR Consultancy Festival—a highly anticipated face-to-face event designed to bring the community together. This festival is an opportunity for members to:

- Connect and build relationships with fellow HR consultants in person
- Attend inspirational talks and workshops led by industry experts
- Participate in interactive sessions covering the latest trends, business growth strategies, and consulting innovations

- Celebrate achievements and share successes within a supportive environment
- Enjoy a mix of learning, networking, and social activities designed to reignite passion and motivation for their consulting journey

The festival is a standout event in the HR consulting calendar, reinforcing the Academy's commitment to continuous development, peer support, and industry excellence.

A Continuous Learning and Growth Experience

Unlike one-off training courses, The HR Consultancy Academy® provides ongoing support throughout every stage of an HR consultant's journey—whether they are just starting or looking to scale their business to new heights. It's a place where consultants can grow their confidence, increase their income, and create the freedom and flexibility they desire in their careers.

By being part of The HR Consultancy Academy®, members no longer feel isolated in their consulting journey—they gain a network, resources, and guidance that empower them to build a thriving, sustainable business.

PART 5:
Living the Dream: The Next Level

"I'VE FOUND THAT LUCK IS QUITE PREDICTABLE. IF YOU WANT MORE LUCK, TAKE MORE CHANCES. BE MORE ACTIVE. SHOW UP MORE OFTEN."

BRIAN TRACY

Chapter 18:
Career transition stories from HR professionals who leaped

In this chapter, five extraordinary people share their stories of how they have made the career transition into HR consulting and the early years.

STORY 1 – NEW CHALLENGES

Bootcamp Success Stories

Angela Senior
Aire Valley Consultancy Ltd

1. Looking Back: My Career Path Before Consulting

My career journey began at Safeway Plc, where I spent six years progressing from HR Manager to Regional HR Operations Manager, overseeing 42 stores along the M62 corridor. Following Safeway's acquisition by Morrisons in 2004, I played a key role in the divestment process but ultimately chose redundancy to focus on family. After a maternity break, I joined a family-run business specialising in nuts, bolts, and power tools—a surprising but valuable 16-year journey. I advanced from HR Manager to HRBP, then Head of HR and Operations, and eventually Operations Director, leaving in January 2024.

I thrived on having a voice in shaping culture, developing leaders, and advocating for employee well-being. However, as the business transitioned from family-led to a more corporate structure, I lost that voice and connection, making it clear that change was necessary.

2. The Leap into Consulting®: My Defining Moment

When my Managing Director left, the company changed rapidly, and I no longer felt aligned with its direction. My confidence wavered—I questioned my abilities and worried that my experience in a single business might not translate to consulting. Instead of diving straight in, I took another job, only to realise within weeks that I was repeating the same cycle—feeling unheard and unfulfilled.

In March, I joined Sarah's HR Consulting Bootcamp, and everything clicked. Surrounded by like-minded professionals and equipped with practical knowledge, I saw a path forward. By April 2024, I quit my job again—this time, for good.

3. Transferable Skills and Unexpected Strengths

Resilience, empathy, and people-first leadership were my strongest assets. But consulting required more than HR expertise. Surprisingly, my business acumen—understanding marketing, sales, financial forecasting, and operational strategy—became invaluable. I could build a P&L, manage cash flow, and apply these insights to my own business.

4. *Breakthrough Moments and Wins*

People made all the difference. The network and Bootcamp community provided unwavering support, and LinkedIn became a game-changer for my visibility. Initially hesitant to share my opinions publicly, I embraced content creation, and soon other HR consultants praised my insights. Imposter syndrome lingered, but seeing clients return, gaining referrals, and being invited onto Sarah's podcast (and now this book!) solidified my success.

My biggest breakthrough? Realising I had a legitimate business—one that was thriving. No longer checking my bank account daily, I built relationships at networking events where seasoned entrepreneurs sought my advice.

5. *The Impact of the HR Consulting Bootcamp*

Bootcamp accelerated my journey. Coming from corporate, many details—like ICO registration or structuring a business—were unfamiliar. Bootcamp provided clarity, saved time, and helped me avoid common pitfalls. The standout lesson? Sarah's 5C's Corporate to Consulting framework, which guided my planning and decision-making. Though I didn't fully grasp it at first, revisiting it as my business evolved gave me confidence and direction.

6. *Lessons in Hindsight: What I'd Do Differently*

I would have trusted myself more. Taking that interim job was unnecessary—I was ready. I also would have stopped comparing myself to others and embraced the learning curve sooner. Fear and failure are just feedback.

Advice for Aspiring Consultants

- **Plan your journey** (5C's) but stay flexible.
- **You won't know everything at first**—and that's okay.
- **Network consistently**—LinkedIn and a strong community are gold.
- **Believe in yourself**—imposter syndrome is normal, but don't let it stop you.
- **Manage your finances early**—business income isn't as predictable as a salary.

Bonus: If client work slows down, work on your business. And remember, it's okay to say no.

7. *Year One: Surprises, Wins, and Challenges*

The biggest surprise? How welcoming the HR consulting community is. Early on, other consultants referred clients to me and offered support. Writing for this book and appearing on a podcast have been unexpected highlights.

Wins included cracking tough client relationships, hitting my Year 1 financial goal in just seven months, and qualifying as a teacher to deliver specialised training in Year 2. The biggest challenge? Wearing *every* hat—IT, finance, marketing, sales. Discussing fees with clients was also a learning curve.

Time management was another hurdle. Balancing financial goals with lifestyle aspirations required careful consideration—I often struggled to say no to referrals because I didn't want to let people down. I now work harder than ever, but I have a plan.

8. *Year Two and Beyond: Strategic Shifts*

As I near the end of my first year, I'm refining my focus—identifying my ideal clients and aligning my business model with my lifestyle goals. I've learned to recognise when clients don't value HR, and I'm building a sustainable approach that prioritises meaningful work over sheer volume.

Year 2 is about courage—putting myself out there, strengthening my brand, and ensuring my long-term business plan is robust and adaptable.

9. *Work-Life Balance: Reality vs. Expectation*

Has consulting provided the freedom I envisioned? In some ways, yes—I've eliminated the Sunday night dread, and I control my schedule. However, I became busy quickly, so the flexibility I imagined hasn't fully materialised yet. But I expected the first few years to be intense, and the difference now is that I work for my goals, my family, and my future.

The best part? Choosing who I work with, working from home, and knowing that, over time, I'll refine the balance even further. Consulting has been the best decision I've ever made.

10. *Final Thought: Take the Leap*

If you're considering consulting, trust yourself. It's a journey, but one worth taking. I'll never look back!

Angela Senior
https://www.linkedin.com/in/angela-senior-avc/

STORY 2 – FINDING YOUR NICHE

Bootcamp Success Stories

Gemma Bromfield
Go Beyond HR Consultancy

1. *Looking Back: The Career Path Before Consulting*

For 22 years, I worked in employment, always sensing that something didn't quite fit. I struggled with aligning to agendas I didn't fully support and resented the rigidity of set working hours. Before being made redundant in October 2021, I was in an HR Partner role, and the urge to carve my own path was growing stronger. The transactional side of HR no longer excited me, and the constraints of structured hours were becoming increasingly difficult to navigate.

2. *The Key Moment: Taking the Leap into Consulting*

While searching for a new job, I wrote down my ideal role criteria. My husband observed, "Gemma, the only way you'll get that is if you're self-employed." That was my golden ticket—the realisation that I could escape the corporate rat race and build something meaningful on my own terms. Consulting offered me the opportunity to make a real impact, pursue accreditation in workplace mediation (a long-held ambition), and break free from the constraints of conformity. My decision was made.

3. Translating Corporate Skills into Consulting Success

The skills I honed in the corporate world laid the foundation for my independent consulting journey. I am grateful for those years—they allowed me to master my craft, earn my CIPD qualification, and identify areas of HR that needed transformation. When I transitioned to self-employment, I embraced the chance to implement those changes and create a business that aligned with my values and aspirations.

4. Breakthrough Moments in the Transition

The defining moment in my transition was discovering Sarah Hamilton-Gill's HR Consulting Bootcamp. It was then that I realised I didn't just want to run a generalist HR consultancy—I wanted to specialise in conflict resolution, an area I am deeply passionate about. That decision ignited a newfound excitement, and I ran with it. It was a risk, but as the saying goes, **"He who dares, wins."**

5. The Impact of the HR Consulting Bootcamp

The HR Consulting Bootcamp was instrumental in shaping my journey. Without it, I doubt I would have successfully launched my business. While I have always had big ideas, I lacked the structure to bring them to life. The Bootcamp provided a clear roadmap, guiding me through the process of setting up a consultancy.

One of the most valuable aspects was the sense of community—I met like-minded individuals, including my now close friend, James Carmen. The wealth of expertise within the Bootcamp was phenomenal. From LinkedIn content creation to accountancy and website development, there was an expert available to support every aspect of the business. Most importantly, Sarah's 30+ years of consulting experience provided invaluable insights into best practices, common pitfalls, and the importance of understanding my "why." The safety net of the Bootcamp made the transition feel far less daunting.

6. *Reflections: What I Would Do Differently*

If I could do it all over again, I would have taken the leap much sooner. My advice to my past self? Just go for it! You don't have to adhere to societal norms. Since becoming self-employed, I have been diagnosed with combined ADHD, which has given me a new perspective on why I struggled with the structure of corporate life. Consulting has allowed me to work in a way that aligns with how my brain operates best.

7. *Top Five Tips for Aspiring Consultants*

- **Plan and Prepare** – Have a clear roadmap and financial buffer for your first year.
- **Join the Bootcamp** – It will set you up for success and support your growth.
- **Build Your Network** – Surround yourself with a strong support system and join networking groups.
- **Be Realistic About Finances** – Business takes time to build, so manage cash flow wisely.
- **Follow Your Passion** – Don't box yourself into work that doesn't excite you; pursue what drives you every day.

8. *The First Year: Surprises, Wins, and Challenges*

My first year in consulting was a rollercoaster. The biggest surprise? How generous and supportive the consulting community is—something I hadn't experienced in corporate life. My greatest win was the growth in my confidence and the ability to live life on my own terms. The biggest challenge was managing cash flow and navigating the uncertainty of securing new business.

9. Evolving in Year Two and Beyond

Year two brought new lessons. I experienced a quiet period, which forced me to reflect deeply and seek advice from fellow consultants. This prompted a shift in strategy, and by the latter half of the year, business picked up significantly. I also recognised the need to take the "business" side of my consultancy more seriously understanding my numbers, tracking trends, and creating financial stability.

Being diagnosed with ADHD and starting medication provided much-needed clarity, helping me focus on tasks essential for profitability. Now, in year three (2025), I have an accountability partnership with James Carmen. Together, we support each other in growing our businesses, tackling the uncomfortable tasks, and pushing ourselves towards greater success.

10. Work-Life Balance and the Reality of Consulting

Consulting has been life changing. I wake up every day excited about my work, surrounded by inspiring people. It has exceeded my expectations in terms of flexibility and autonomy.

Flexibility for me means structuring my day in a way that suits my natural rhythms. I rarely schedule meetings before 10 am, as my mornings are reserved for personal rituals. I have designed my office to reflect my personality and needs—a heated chair because I hate the cold, a speaker for my reggae playlists, and cherished photos of my loved ones.

11. *The biggest benefit?*

- No longer needing permission to take time off.
- No rigid dress codes.
- No exhausting commutes.

Consulting has given me the freedom to live and work on my own terms, and I wouldn't trade it for anything.

Gemma Bromfield
https://www.linkedin.com/in/gemma-bromfield/

STORY 3 – SCALING FOR SUCCESS

Bootcamp Success Stories

Jaclyn Pringle
HR Staple Ltd®

1. *Looking back, what was your career path before stepping into consulting?*

Before making the move into consulting, my career followed a relatively linear path in HR for over 15 years. I landed my first HR role at the age of 20 and steadily progressed into more senior positions, consciously choosing opportunities that allowed me to experience a variety of organisational cultures—across public, private, and not-for-profit sectors. These roles gave me a breadth of exposure that became invaluable later on.

2. *What did you enjoy (or not enjoy) about your previous role?*

I genuinely enjoyed the roles I held and the wealth of experience they provided—especially leading teams and working on strategic HR initiatives. It was fascinating to see how different leadership styles and workplace cultures influenced team dynamics. What really lit me up was the chance to see great HR in action—how it could truly transform an organisation and its people. On the other hand, I found less enjoyment in the more reactive, firefighting side of HR.

3. *What was the key moment or realisation that made you take the leap into consulting?*

There wasn't a single lightbulb moment—it was more of a slow burn. The idea of consulting had been on my mind for a while, but like many people, I hesitated. It felt like a big leap, and it was easy to find reasons not to move forward. But after years in senior HR roles, an MSc in HR Management, and achieving Chartered Fellow status with the CIPD, I began to feel equipped—and ready. I wanted to make strategic HR more accessible to SMEs and loved the idea of working with a diverse range of clients, each seeking high-quality HR support. This growing desire led me to join the HR Consulting Bootcamp. The confidence and clarity I gained there helped me finally make the decision to launch. I picked a 'go-live' date and built my plans from there.

4. *Which skills from your corporate role have been most valuable in your consulting journey?*

Without a doubt, the range of experience I gained across different types of organisations proved incredibly useful. As a consultant, you never know what your next enquiry will be, and having that varied background to draw on made a huge difference. It gave me the confidence to handle a broad spectrum of challenges.

5. *Thinking about your transition into consulting, what were your biggest wins or breakthrough moments?*

The transition itself was both exciting and uncomfortable—but that's exactly where the growth happened. One of the early breakthrough moments was pitching against much larger, more established consultancies—and winning. That was a huge confidence boost and proved that the quality of my offer could stand shoulder to shoulder with the best.

6. *How did the HR Consulting Bootcamp shape your journey?*

The Bootcamp was a game-changer. It was enjoyable, practical, and incredibly reassuring to meet others going through the same transition. Consulting can feel isolating at first, and the Bootcamp offered a real sense of community. The content helped me get my ducks in a row and launch with confidence. I'm certain that solid foundation was a key part of my successful start.

7. *If you could go back and do it all over again, would you take a different approach?*

I wouldn't change much, but if I could offer my past self one piece of advice, it would be this: start speaking your clients' language sooner. I had been so used to talking in HR terms, but in consulting, it's about showing the commercial value—how your work impacts the business. Get clear on what clients really want and don't be afraid to confidently share your value. Don't hold back.

8. *What are your top five pieces of advice for someone considering leaving employment to start their own consulting business?*

- **Get comfortable being uncomfortable**—it's a big shift and there's a steep learning curve.
- **Build a support network early on**—it can be lonely, and having people in the same boat is invaluable.
- **Be clear on your services and goals**—but also know that true clarity comes from taking action.
- **Progress over perfection**—don't wait until everything's perfect to get started.
- **It will be full-on**—there's always something to do, so boundaries and downtime are key.

9. *Your first year as a consultant – what were the biggest surprises, wins, and challenges?*

The first year went incredibly well. I became known for delivering high-quality HR support and quickly secured several retained clients. Feedback was consistently positive, which helped build momentum. One standout moment was becoming a finalist for 'New Business of the Year' at the local Chamber of Commerce awards—a proud and affirming achievement.

On the flip side, one of the biggest challenges was finding time to implement the right systems and processes—things like finance, CRM, time tracking, and email marketing. When you're busy with client work, it's tough to carve out the time to build those foundations properly. Wearing all the different hats was definitely a stretch—especially in areas I wasn't naturally interested in.

10. *As your business evolved in year two and beyond, were there any major turning points, lessons, or strategic shifts?*

A major turning point came when I realised the business needed to grow beyond just me. I hadn't used associates, but demand was increasing, and to maintain the quality and scale the business, I made the decision to hire. It was a big move—but the right one. It allowed the business to grow sustainably while upholding the high standards I'd built my reputation on.

11. *How has consulting impacted your work-life balance? Has it lived up to your expectations, and what does flexibility look like for you now?*

Work-life balance is a bit of a moving target. I've always been client-focused, and in the early days, that meant not always setting the best boundaries. I've come to realise how important it is to actually book time off and take it—your own wellbeing matters too. While it's easy to let your own needs slip down the list, one of the biggest benefits of consulting is the flexibility. I sometimes forget just how much freedom I have now compared to my corporate life—but I'm hugely grateful for it. Making the leap in 2021 was absolutely the right decision.

Jaclyn Pringle
https://www.linkedin.com/in/jaclynpringle/

STORY 4 – FLEXIBILITY

Bootcamp Success Stories

James Carman
365 People Support

1. Looking Back: My Career Path Before Consulting

Over two decades of operations management running a variety of single and multi-site hospitality businesses across the UK and Australia shaped my journey. I thrived on the team effort of turning around underperforming businesses, the camaraderie that came with it, and the fast-paced problem-solving that hospitality demands. I also found immense fulfilment in training, developing, and coaching managers to achieve their goals—knowing that many of them continue to successfully run venues on both sides of the world is incredibly rewarding.

2. The Moment I Took the Leap into Consulting

After the first lockdown, I stepped away from operations. As I reviewed my CV, I realised that coaching, training, and developing people had been central to my career. Wanting to continue down that path, I pursued a Master's in International Human Resource

Management to transition into an HR role where I could continue to develop individuals. At the same time, I undertook the ILM Level 5 in Coaching and Mentoring to complement my practical experience with a recognised qualification.

I started applying for roles but kept getting knocked back—my lack of HR department experience seemed to be a barrier. That's when I decided to take matters into my own hands and launch a business supporting hospitality companies with HR, coaching, and mentoring. And so, 365 People Support was born in November 2021.

3. The Skills That Made the Difference

My experience running businesses gave me an edge that many starting out in consulting struggle with. I understood the importance of networking, marketing, resilience, and the need for persistence. I also knew not to rely on a single revenue stream—I needed income from multiple sources, including contacts, networking, associate work, and direct marketing.

Without a traditional HR department background, I leaned into my extensive operational experience in people management. At the same time, I had to quickly learn the nuances of HR that I hadn't previously needed to navigate in my operational roles.

4. Breakthrough Moments in Consulting

My biggest win was discovering the HR Consulting Bootcamp. Another HR consultant on LinkedIn recommended Sarah Hamilton-Gill's book, and her experiences resonated deeply with me. After reading it, I reached out to Sarah. It took me a while to take the plunge, but enrolling in the Bootcamp gave me clarity—and, more importantly, a community. The relationships I built there have been invaluable. My fellow consultants and I regularly bounce ideas off each other, and their guidance has helped me navigate unfamiliar territory, such as dealing with unions, which were never a factor in the hospitality sector.

5. *The HR Consulting Bootcamp's Impact*

The Bootcamp was a game-changer. Beyond the practical knowledge, it provided a support network that made all the difference. The community aspect alone has been worth its weight in gold.

6. *If I Could Do It All Over Again*

I would tell my past self not to compare my journey to others. Early on, I couldn't understand why some consultants seemed to achieve success faster than I did. I also wish I had been more mindful of my spending—I invested heavily upfront in things like a website, Extended DISC practitioner status, and partnerships, which depleted my financial cushion sooner than I anticipated.

While I niched into hospitality from the start, I now wonder if that initial focus may have hindered me. I pushed the hospitality theme hard and may have inadvertently limited my opportunities with other industries like IT or engineering. I also underestimated how long it would take for the hospitality sector—going through immense upheaval at the time—to recognize the need for external HR support.

7. *Five Key Pieces of Advice for Aspiring Consultants*

- Be patient. Success takes time. I was advised it could take six months to gain enough clients to sustain the business, but for me, it took over a year.
- **Avoid comparison.** Social media isn't a true reflection of people's journeys—behind the success stories are struggles and setbacks that aren't always visible.

- **Line up some work before you take the leap.** The early days can be demotivating if you're just posting on LinkedIn and attending webinars without tangible projects to work on.
- **Find someone to talk to who understands.** A fellow consultant, especially one further along in the journey, can provide the kind of support that partners or family members may not fully grasp.
- **Don't wait for perfection.** I used to tell my managers, "Excellence over perfection every time," but I didn't follow my own advice early on. Procrastination over perfecting social media posts and other tasks slowed me down—it's something I still battle with today.

8. Year One: Surprises, Wins, and Challenges

The biggest surprise? How long it took to get going. Another surprise was that my first significant projects came from contacts I hadn't spoken to in over a decade.

Biggest win? The Bootcamp, as well as completing an investigation course with TCM and joining their consultant partner network.

Biggest challenge? Staying positive when work wasn't coming in, but expenses were piling up.

9. Evolving in Year Two and Beyond

At the start of year two, I realised I needed a mindset shift. A fellow Bootcamper coached me through it, and as my confidence improved, so did my business. She continues to be my go-to person when I have wobbles—though thankfully, they are becoming less frequent.

10. Work-Life Balance and Flexibility

I market myself as available 365 days a year, 24/7, to align with the needs of my hospitality clients. In reality, I don't receive many out-of-hours calls, so my working hours are much lighter than they were in the industry. I now earn a similar income to what I did in full-time employment, but for a fraction of the hours—which means I still have plenty of capacity for growth.

Flexibility is one of the biggest wins. Working from home means no commute, and thanks to the widespread acceptance of video calls, I now have clients across the country, rather than just within my local area.

Work-life balance? Excellent.
Flexibility? Outstanding.

James Carman
https://www.linkedin.com/in/jamescarman121/

STORY 5 - CARVING MY OWN PATH

Bootcamp Success Stories

Lindy Hoyt
People Ambassadors

1. *Looking back, what was your career path before stepping into consulting? What did you enjoy (or not enjoy) about your previous role?*

My career in HR spanned almost two decades, with a focus on Strategic Partnerships. I started as an HR Coordinator and steadily worked my way up to becoming an HR Director. What truly lit me up about the work was the people—supporting individuals, building better workplace cultures, and partnering with leaders to make a real impact.

I was fortunate to work alongside an incredible HR leader who shaped not only my career but who I am today. She championed her team and had a unique ability to bring out the best in those around her. Thank you, Lori for believing in me.

Over the years, I experienced the full spectrum of leadership. Some leaders I worked with shared my values, while others didn't. Those misalignments were pivotal—they helped me get clear on what

I stood for. And sometimes, the bravest thing you can do is walk away, when your values are no longer aligned with the culture. That moment felt both bold and liberating.

2. *What was the key moment or realisation that made you take the leap into consulting?*

It wasn't one single moment—it was a gradual build-up over time. Eventually, I found myself at a fork in the road and thought, "What if I took the other path? What if I took a chance on me?"

I craved a space where I could work with people who shared my values, where I could create my table instead of asking for a seat at someone else's. I wanted to design a business that fit around my life—not the other way around.

When I became pregnant with my second child, my daughter, it felt like a turning point. I paused and asked myself, "What do I truly want?" That question wasn't easy to answer—but it was necessary. Listening to the Leap into HR Consulting® podcast helped me see what was possible. Hearing others share their journeys lit a spark in me—I knew I could do it too.

3. *Which skills from your corporate role have been most valuable in your consulting journey? Have any unexpected skills come in handy?*

Listening. Really listening. Not just to respond—but to understand. That's been my superpower in consulting. It's not about quick fixes; it's about meeting clients where they are and helping them build workplaces where everyone can thrive.

Communication planning and negotiation have also been critical—whether it's shaping client engagements, navigating expectations, or supporting leaders through tough calls. I lean on those skills daily.

4. *Thinking about your transition into consulting, what were your biggest wins or breakthrough moments?*

One of the biggest revelations was just how many businesses truly need help. I work primarily with small and medium-sized companies that don't have an in-house HR team. They don't know what they don't know—and I get to be the person who guides and supports them through the ups and downs of both business and life.

5. *How did the HR Consulting Bootcamp shape your journey? Were there any standout lessons or game-changing insights?*

Community. That was the standout for me. Being on the journey with others who were also making the leap into consulting made all the difference. We learned from one another, shared the highs and lows, and formed bonds that have lasted far beyond the Bootcamp itself.

Another huge insight was clarity. The structure, the questions, and the space to reflect helped me get crystal clear on where I wanted to go. And once you know where you're headed, the path becomes much easier to navigate.

6. *If you could go back and do it all over again, would you take a different approach? What advice would you give your past self?*

I'd remind myself to trust the process. You don't need to have everything figured out from day one. Things will evolve. Keep pivoting until it feels right—that's how growth happens.

7. *What are your top five pieces of advice for someone considering leaving employment to start their own consulting business?*

- **Trust yourself and your experience.** Your corporate background is more than enough—it will carry you.

- **Follow your instincts.** They'll never lead you wrong.
- **Expect to feel scared.** That's normal. Fear means you're growing.
- **Have a plan, but don't wait for the "perfect" time.** It doesn't exist.
- **Just do it.** You'll never regret trying—but you *will* regret wondering "what if."

8. *Your first year as a consultant – what were the biggest surprises, wins, and challenges?*

I landed my first two pitches—and they were *big* projects. That gave me a strong start and affirmed I was on the right path. But the biggest realization was this: running your own business is the ultimate personal development journey. It never ends. And if you love learning, it's the best kind of adventure.

9. *How has consulting impacted your work-life balance? Has it lived up to your expectations, and what does flexibility look like for you now?*

My life is so much richer now. I have time to breathe, to think, to cook dinners and go on walks with my husband. I can show up fully at my children's events and fully present in the evenings and on weekends.

The business is thriving—but what truly lights me up is the life I get to lead because of it. And that, to me, is the real success story.

Lindy Hoyt
https://www.linkedin.com/in/lindy-peterson-phr/

TOP TIPS ABOUT A CAREER TRANSITION:

Look before you leap
Try consulting part time before committing fully to leaving if this is an option.

Save up for your dream lifestyle
Live below your means before you leave your corporate job and save as much as you can, knowing that your business may take time to be profitable. We suggest having a 3 month safety net in the bank.

Follow your passion
Do work that is mostly enjoyable to you, rather than the work you have had to do in the corporate world.

Transition well
Be kind to yourself as you adapt to your new identity, new time commitments, and new levels of income. Take time to smell the roses and enjoy the control you have over your time. Be patient!

When will you make a career transition?

A new day - a new dawn

THE POWER OF FEEDBACK

In addition to the stories you have just read, we have continuous feedback from our clients across the range of services we offer.

You may think that feedback is a process that businesses go through just to prove they have happy clients.

I have just sat reading a bootcamp feedback form and it brought me to tears. I am changing people's lives by enabling them to have more flexibility, fun, income, and purpose.

As a consultant this is my barometer of how well I am delivering my services and whether they are the right services.

A few years ago, I met an entrepreneur with a business designed around collecting feedback for their clients. They specialise in a number of sectors and we discussed how this could work for my business.

As many of my services are online it has become even more important for social proofing that potential clients can see verified feedback. I commissioned Working Feedback to collaborate with us to do this.

Working Feedback

We incorporate the links to the feedback on all key media and ask for feedback after events and coaching. The data collected through the system then generates statistics and reports for us to review monthly and we are given a certificate each month.

We can use these five-star reviews to share on social media. In addition to this we also see feedback from the clients on what other services they would be interested in. It's a great way to get referrals and to track conversion rates.

They are also published on our home page of our website and added to our social proofing strategy that I talked about in the chapter on Credibility.

CERTIFICATE OF ACHIEVEMENT

WorkingFeedback — VERIFIED RATING

THIS CERTIFICATE IS PRESENTED TO

Leap into Consulting

★★★★★

FOR ACHIEVING A 98% RECOMMENDATION RATING FROM FEEDBACK
This rating has been recorded and independently verified by Working Feedback, a third party review service.

ACHIEVED FOR THE MONTH OF
March 2025

To see the most recent reviews visit
https://my.workingfeedback.co.uk/hr-consultants/lymington/leapintoconsulting.com

Chapter 19: Remember the dream

My dream was to live and work in Corfu, Greece – and I've made it happen. I write this closing chapter while enjoying Greek cheese and coffee in my home just a few minutes' walk from Messonghi village, overlooking the sea towards the Greek mainland.

I did this by creating a consulting career that worked around my personal needs and desires. It freed me from the office ties, brought in a salary to exceed anything I ever earned while working the 9-5, and allowed me to choose not only how much I worked, but also when I worked.

I could talk about my new life in Corfu for hours, but mine is one dream, of many. It's time to refocus on what you want from your journey as a consultant.

WHAT IS YOUR DREAM?

What steps are you taking to get there?

Maybe it's the opportunity to work on more exciting projects? To bring in a higher income allowing you to take more holidays? To spend more time with family? Or perhaps, like me, you wish to move your life abroad to somewhere with a more moderate climate. Winters in the UK and summers in Greece, anyone?

All of this, and much, much more is possible when you take the Leap into HR Consulting®. As someone who has made it happen, trust me when I tell you that you can do it.

My business model works – I'm living proof of it and I want to help others achieve it.

That's why I offer coaching, short courses, bootcamps, and retreats all designed to allow you the opportunity to follow your dreams and have continuous development focused exclusively on consulting skills.

The team and I would love to inspire and guide you on your consulting journey.

No two journeys are the same.

If you haven't already signed up for the bonuses, go to this link and join our community:

https://leap-into-consulting.mykajabi.com/Book-Downloads

What are you waiting for?

Make the Leap into HR Consulting® today.

Enjoy your journey!

Sarah Hamilton-Gill
LEAP INTO HR CONSULTING

About the Author

Sarah Hamilton-Gill FCIPD – Visionary Mentor & Trailblazer in HR Consulting

There are two dynamic sides to Sarah Hamilton-Gill FCIPD—the strategic business leader and the adventurous free spirit. As a renowned entrepreneur, executive coach, public speaker, and best-selling author, Sarah is widely recognised as the UK's leading mentor for HR professionals transitioning into consulting.

A Career Defined by Innovation & Impact

Sarah's journey began with a fast rise through the corporate ranks, becoming the youngest HR Manager at Sainsbury's at just 24. From there, she worked with household names such as Owen Owen, Dorothy Perkins, and Foster Menswear before making the bold decision in 1994 to leave corporate life and launch her own HR consultancy.

Over the past 30 years, Sarah has worked with hundreds of organisations and thousands of HR professionals, helping them navigate business growth, leadership, and transformation. She has a deep understanding of what makes businesses tick—a crucial skill when working with CEOs and founders.

Her pioneering work in HR consulting has earned her multiple industry accolades, including being named one of the HR Most Influential Thinkers. She has also been recognised as a finalist for the Business Woman of the

Year Awards and continues to be a sought-after thought leader in the HR space.

Founder of Leap into HR Consulting® & The HR Consultancy Academy®

Sarah's passion for empowering others led her to create the Leap into HR Consulting® brand, helping over 250+ HR professionals launch their own consultancies. During the pandemic alone, she successfully guided over 50 HR professionals to pivot their careers, demonstrating her resilience and ability to navigate change.

Today, she continues to inspire and support HR professionals through The HR Consultancy Academy®, offering expert guidance, mentoring, and a supportive community to those ready to take control of their careers.

Living Life with Passion & Purpose

Beyond her business success, Sarah embraces freedom and adventure. Corfu is her spiritual home, where she recharges, often behind the lens of her camera capturing the island's beauty. She's also an avid water sports enthusiast—her claim to fame? Representing England in underwater hockey and winning against France!

As a mother of two grown-up sons, Sarah has mastered the art of balancing business with life's joys. If you contact her on a Friday, she might be out sailing the Ionian Sea or hiking a mountain—but come Monday, she's ready to help you build your dream consulting business.

Connect with Sarah:

Podcast Host of Leap into HR Consulting®

Sarah Hamilton-Gill FCIPD
www.linkedin.com/in/sarahhg

www.leapintoconsulting.com

For information on The HR Consultancy Academy® please got to :
www.thehrconsultancyacademy.com

Please share your feedback about this book on Amazon.

References and Thanks for Contributions

1. To review the full report from UK Small Business Statistics (2024 Update) https://www.fsb.org.uk/media-centre/uk-small-business-statistics

2. For further reading on VUCA, see https://hbr.org/2014/01/what-vuca-really-means-for-you

3. *Psychology Today* article available at https://www.psychologytoday.com/us/basics/confidence

4. One Bad Review Is All It Takes, *Harvard Business Review*, Jul/Aug 2020, Vol. 98 Issue 4, p.22.

5. This publicly available information is used under licence as outlined here: https://www.nationalarchives.gov.uk/doc/open-government-licence/version/3/

6. For more information on Dr Elisabeth Kübler-Ross' work, see https://www.psycom.net/depression.central.grief.html

There are many people that have contributed to my thinking along my journey, both personally and on a business basis. Our community is amazing and there are so many people I am grateful to for believing in me.

Thanks to the team at Globus HR Consulting Ltd along with our partners and our HR profession worldwide. We will continue to support the unique needs of our HR consulting community.

ADDITIONAL RESOURCES

To see more information, and our news and events:
www.leapintoconsulting.com

To gain additional resources mentioned throughout the book please head across to:
https://leap-into-consulting.mykajabi.com/products/book-downloads